# LIVE
## ABUNDANTLY!
### BUSINESS LESSONS FROM THE
## BIBLE

# F. E. TABOR

ISBN: 145631159X
ISBN-13: 9781456311599

Thank you to all my friends and relatives who have helped me so many times.

And a very special

# Thank You!

To our Heavenly Father, who brought them into my life.

# PERSONAL NOTE TO MY READER:

Life is not a river to passively float down. It is a mountain to be climbed. As every good mountaineer knows, sometimes it is necessary to go down, to reach a better route to the top.

God is the guide who can see our path from the sky.

Back when my small business thrived, I wrote the first version of this book. A friend said, "Fran, this will be a message to yourself." Those words proved prophetic.

For the next two years, the vibrant economy poured money into my business. I abandoned my own guiding principles.

Unlike Joseph's pharaoh, those years of plenty did not leave me wealthy. I entered the lean years deeply in debt.

I re-discovered my book; remembered its inspiration. These principles again guide my business.

Re-discovering The Best Business Book, God's Word, helped my floundered business recover.

Because of these principles, my business became more profitable in a recession than it was during the time of plenty.


This book has been tested.
Not following these lessons: poverty.
Following them: a way out of poverty.

# CONTENTS

## Introduction

## PART 1
## Elephants to Tithing

# PART II
# Top dog is just a dog

# PART III
## Busyness To Business

# PART IV
# The more we grow, the more we need others.

# PART V
# Life gets Complicated

# INTRODUCTION

## "To live abundantly..."
## Do you want that in writing?

Many sadder-but-wiser business people have learned the hard way, the more important the deal, the more important it is to have it in writing.

God agrees.

That is why we have His Written Word.

In both the Old and New Testaments, God repeatedly promises that if we follow His laws, we will live abundantly. If His laws are not followed, the result will be an earthly as well as a spiritual ruin. For thousands of years, events prove that following God's laws generate true success.

Can following God's laws still generate abundance today?

Too often, as Job observed, it seems the wicked are blessed. Life's unfairness is the focus of many songs and stories.

"Oh Lord, would it spoil some vast, immortal plan if I were a wealthy man?" Pleads the impoverished *Fiddler on the Roof* father of five girls in rural, czarist Russia.

In real life, unfair edicts and poverty drove thousands like him to America, where they created new wealth for both themselves and their new country.

The wealthy, the politically favored, had little reason to leave mother Russia. The "lucky ones" stayed behind, many

1

millions to die of starvation in Stalin's Russia, and millions more from the German invasion during World War II.

The answer to the question "Would it spoil some vast immortal plan if I were a wealthy man?" was a resounding "YES."

The Bible is full of stories of bad luck really being GOOD fortune.

Bad Luck. Joseph is sold into slavery.

Good luck. Joseph's owner makes him the master overseer.

Bad luck. The master's wife attempts to seduce him.

More bad luck. The master believes Joseph attacked his wife.

Good luck. Joseph is allowed to live.

Bad luck. Joseph is thrown into prison.

Good luck. Joseph becomes the master prisoner.

More Good luck. He befriends a prisoner who knows pharaoh. His new friend promises to put in a good word for Joseph.

Bad luck. Once his "friend" is free, he forgets all about Joseph.

Good Luck. After two years, the friend finally remembers Joseph.

Very good luck. Joseph ends up Head Honcho of Egypt, saves his family and helps them move to the safety of Egypt.

All because Joseph was "lucky" enough to be sold into slavery by his own brothers.

In every situation, no matter how bleak, Joseph's response was that it was the will of God. He honored God by being honorable; he gave the Lord credit for all accomplishments and abilities. If instead he had concentrated on the unfairness of it all, whining "Why me?" he would have been just another forgotten foreign slave.

Joseph chose faith.

Our ultimate fortunes are not determined by what happens to us. The sun rises *on the evil and on the good, and it rains on the just and the unjust.*[1]

Our lives are determined by how we choose to react to what happens to us.

No matter how great the unfairness, how repulsive the evil, God sees us not as victims, but as victors.

Victims wait passively to be rescued.

Victors take action, most importantly spiritual action.

Action, especially when the odds are stacked against you, takes faith.

Faith, like any skill, increases only when it is exercised.

There **is** a vast, immortal plan for each and every one of us.

We need to **choose** to have faith in the Planner.

If we have faith in Him, we will have faith in His all-purpose guide for every aspect of life, the Holy Bible.

It makes no difference if you are a nomadic herder tracking your wealth with notches on your walking stick, or a modern CEO with an advanced super computer, business is exchanging goods and services with our follow men. It is people dealing with people.

The Bible gives us rules for dealing with our follow man.

What follows are fifty of the business lessons I have gleaned from His Ultimate Business Book

# PART 1

# ELEPHANTS TO TITHING

Before we can become wealth creators, we need to learn the REAL basics.

# LESSON ONE
## Elephant for Supper!

"How do you eat an elephant?"
    "One bite at a time."

God did not create the earth all at once. He did it in six logical stages, each preparing for the next.[2]

If even He felt it unwise to do everything at once, we shouldn't expect to do so either.

Big complicated jobs are best broken down into smaller segments.

# LESSON TWO
## Toot your own horn! *Silently*

*And God saw everything He had made, and behold it was very good.*[3]

God made a wonderful universe. Of course he could admire His handiwork and declare, "Wow! Those galaxies, the planets, just look at those marvelous whales...it is all so beautiful!" He's God, He's perfect, His creation is perfect, but what about us mere humans?

Dare we pretend anything we do is good enough to say to ourselves, "I did *good!*"

Many of us have been taught it is conceit—self-love—that enables someone to recognize his natural abilities. We should never acknowledge our accomplishments; we must be blind to our gifts. Worse, we should "humbly" focus only on our failings.

*Even a child is known by his doings, whether his work be...right. The hearing ear, the seeing eye, the Lord hath made.*[4]

We have been given the gift of discernment, eyes and ears to judge if we have done well or badly.

When, with child-like honesty, we self-acknowledge a task well-done, we feel joyously good. ....*he that is of*

9

*a merry heart hath a continuous feast.*[5] *...A merry heart doeth good like a medicine...*[6]

If we do not acknowledge the talents God has given us, how can we give thanks for them? To belittle His gifts, is to belittle the Giver.

To not use those gifts, is an even bigger insult to the Giver.

Why not shout from the roof tops, "Thank you, God, for letting me be wonderful!"

The line between happiness from an accomplishment and vanity's abusive self-love is dangerously thin. Whenever we deliberately invite the praise of others, that line is crossed.

A private prayer of thankfulness helps keep us from crossing that line.

A big advantage to not publicly bragging, is that it helps prevent humiliation.

*Boast not of thyself of tomorrow; for thou knowest not what the day may bring forth. Let another man praise thee, and not thy own mouth; a stranger and not thy own lips.*[7]

We each have an obligation to look for opportunities to be that praising stranger.

When we praise another's accomplishments, we are also praising the One who makes all things wonderful possible.

# LESSON THREE
## Diligent Laziness

*...and He rested on the seventh day from all the work which he had made.*[8]

If God, the all-powerful, felt it necessary to rest on the seventh day, we mere mortals should not be surprised we also need rest. God believed that rest is so important that in an era without refrigerators, "quikmarts", and microwave ovens *everyone* was to get the seventh day off. No one was allowed to "fudge" by forcing someone else to work for him.

This complete relaxation after a hard week's work wasn't called sloth; it was called devotion.

In our modern competitive world, taking a day off can seem as senseless as a race car driver stopping in the middle of the Indy 500.

With the finish line in sight, it can be tempting to think there are enough fumes in the tank to not risk loosing the lead. If the "winning" car's fumes run out just inches before the finish line, the time he saved not getting that last refill is as useless to him as the dust kicked up by the winner's tires.

When we are busy working, our minds are full with the worries of this world. We are spending our emotional and spiritual energy faster than a racing car consumes gasoline.

11

It is only when we take a break from the many demands of business that we can truly be at rest.

*Be still; and know that I am God.*[9]

When we force ourselves to be still, it allows us to be aware of God's spirit; to let His energy enter our souls like gasoline filling up a car.

# LESSON FOUR
# The Emergency Masquerade

Business owners suffer from a special vanity temptation. We are important to our businesses. Sometimes, we just "know" that if we don't do an extra bit of work on our Day of Rest, our financial world will crash.

There are tasks so important that, if left undone, our worry will make rest impossible.

When challenged about the lawfulness of healing on the Sabbath, Christ replied

*"...What man shall be among you, that shall have a sheep, and if it fall into a pit on the Sabbath Day, will not lay hold on it, and lift it out?"*[10]

*"...the Sabbath was made for man, and not man for the Sabbath..."*[11]

If in doubt about the true degree of urgency, we can ask God.

A wise parent, He often answers, "If you have to ask, it really isn't all that urgent, is it?"

# LESSON FIVE
## KIS Your Mission Statement

When the Israelites first heard all the many daily rules Moses dictated to them, they enthusiastically promised to follow God's laws.[12]

Even as they shouted, "Yes! We will obey!" some may have wondered, "What kind of hoops am I expected to jump through just to get through a day?"

Others may have feared, "There is no way I can memorize all those rules piled on rules!"

Some may have smugly believed, "Now I know everything I need to know to be holy. Perfection, here I come."

Even with all those pages of rules, not every possible situation could be covered. How could any ordinary man tell if a given activity qualified as allowed or forbidden?

God Himself answered that question. He proclaimed a Mission Statement to guide his Chosen People:

*For I am the Lord, your God; ye shall therefore sanctify yourselves, and ye shall be holy; for I am holy...*[13]

With that simple mission statement, all it takes to determine the desirability of a given activity, is to ask if the activity brings one closer to God (being holy), or farther from God (being unclean, or less holy). It is God's litmus test.

15

When Jonah went to the city of Nin-e-veh, he warned the people that God would destroy them if they didn't repent.

A miracle happened. From the king on down, everyone repented! Hallelujah!

*But it displeased Jonah exceedingly and he was very angry.*[14]

Jonah had eagerly looked forward to city-destroying fireworks. Now he had to settle for watching a humbled people coming to God.

Nothing in Leviticus explicitly tells how to behave if a whole city repents, yet God punished Jonah.

Why?

God's simple, unambiguous mission statement said, "Be holy, for I am holy."

It would have been more God-like to rejoice in Nin-e-veh's salvation.

All mission statements should be just as simple, just as unambiguous.

Only then can your mission statement easily serve as a litmus test for the proper actions for both owners and employees in our unpredictable world.

All good mission statements will line up with God's Word.

A mission statement must be attainable.

At first glance God's Mission Statement appears unattainable since no mere mortal can ever hope to be as holy as God. Fortunately for us, He states to Peter

*"What God hath cleansed, that call not thou common."*[15]

His forgiveness makes being holy possible.

A KIS—Keep it Simple—mission statement defines the master goal. It empowers employees (and yourself!) to

16

make on-the-spot decisions without having to run blindly to a rule book.

A KIS mission statement prevents "following the letter of the law" while avoiding the spirit of the law.

Laws written by us imperfect humans often create quagmires of unintended consequences.

For instance, most fast food restaurants have the rule "no food until it is paid for" and a mission statement "Make eating here such a fun family time, everyone will want to come back and spend more money."

Imagine a family at the counter ordering, and their small, very hungry child is fussy. The employee who asks the parent's permission to give the toddler a couple French fries before even taking their order, will break a rule, but accomplish the master goal. The mission statement empowered him to make that judgment call.

Compare that to a beleaguered parent asking an employee at another restaurant, "Could my two-year old have some crackers before we order?" being told "No, not until everything's ordered and paid for."

Which restaurant is more apt to have the family return?

Which will be more profitable that day, and in the future?

Personal experience:

One lovely spring day while driving to Polson, Montana, I saw an old car come barreling out of a side road and broadside the driver's door of the sedan ahead of me.

Both cars spun circles.

Both landed in the ditch.

Street signs and stop signs lay flattened behind them.

Tires squealing, I slammed on my brakes and pulled over.

While calling 911 on my cell phone, I raced to the assaulted sedan.

Front and side airbags had deployed. The elderly couple in the car seemed unhurt, but their vehicle was totaled.

Sirens sounded. Volunteer firemen, first aid crews and highway patrol arrived on the scene. The county sheriff soon followed.

The lady who raced across the highway at sixty miles an hour without looking wasn't drunk, just late for work. Again. Her seatbelt protected her from serious injuries.

We soon learned the elderly couple was from the Netherlands "enjoying" a lifetime-planned retirement vacation touring the United States. They drove a car rented from one of the Glacier International Airport car rental agencies, about seventy miles north.

The couple was headed south to explore western Montana.

He spoke very little English; her English skills were of the academic variety. She could read and understand the rental agreement's fine print, but spoke with a very strong accent.

Both had obvious difficulty understanding us Montanans.

Missoula, Montana, about sixty miles south of Polson, had the closest car rental office.

Since the couple was already heading south to Missoula, we decided to contact the car rental company's Missoula office rather than the originating office. Acting as their phone interpreter, I called the rental company to let them know the couple needed a new vehicle, but not to worry about how they would get to Missoula. I would give them a ride.

The Missoula office manager said, "I cannot authorize a new rental car unless they turn in the old one."

Me, "You don't understand. The old one is totaled. Your head office authorized a local tow truck to take it to a Polson garage. It may never be drivable."

Manager, "Only a senior manager can authorize giving a car without a replacement car. It's Sunday. He won't be in until tomorrow."

The highway patrol man, the sheriff, the fire chief, the tow truck driver, each repeated that the damaged car wasn't leaving Polson.

The manager never wavered. "No old car, no new car."

The sheriff sputtered something inappropriate for this book, finishing with, "No one in my family will ever use your company."

The other emergency responders agreed.

I called the rental office at Glacier International Airport, hoping that since the Glacier office had rented the car, maybe that office could help the Missoula manager develop a little common sense.

I explained the situation.

The Glacier Airport manager sacrificed his Sunday afternoon to help the couple. Arranging for someone to follow him, he drove a replacement rental car south while I drove the elderly couple and all their luggage north. He met us halfway.

After the elderly couple was safely on their way, I asked the young man, "Was the Missoula manager really required to have the couple show up with the wrecked rental car to get a replacement?"

I expected him to say the Missoula manager was severely incompetent.

He answered, "Those are the rules. But as soon as you described what happened, I pictured my parents stranded in a small town in a foreign country because some jackass company insisted on an all-powerful rule book."

He refused to let an inflexible rule book prevent him from doing the right thing.

The real world will create situations we cannot anticipate. A guiding mission statement allows people to respond to the unexpected.

"No return car, no new car issued," is a logical rule.... most of the time.

"Helping customers travel safely with reliable rental cars," should have been the mission all the time.

Requiring an elderly couple to spend the night with a towed and totaled car because they were "required not to leave the vehicle in the care of others," was neither safe for the couple nor good for the company's image.

The lack of an empowering mission statement reduced the rental firm's future income.

# LESSON SIX
# Roofs and Basements

If God's only goal were to have His people living fat and happy in the Promised Land, they would never have left. Everyone would have sat around like so many decadent pet animals waiting for their daily manna from heaven.

He wanted his people to be strong; have a strong sense of identity, a strong belief in His power, a strong desire for His blessings.

He needed a worthy Chosen People to live in the Chosen Land.

From the day Moses returned to Egypt, to the day he saw the Promised Land; his main goal was to return God's People to their home. There were many lesser goals, each one necessary to support the others.

In a similar fashion, a builder's mission statement might be "To create the most beautiful homes ever."

He then might have the long range goal "To build a home for the Smith's"; followed by short range goals such as "dig a basement", "a copper roof", "electrical system."

It is not always easy to tell if a given goal is more like a roof or a basement; only that it is necessary.

It is essential to continuously ask ourselves "What other activities does this support?" "Which support it?"

# LESSON SEVEN
## Money and Shovels

Money is a tool.

As simple a tool as a shovel can illustrate rules for handling money.

If someone gives you a shiny new garden shovel, and you leave it lying in a mud puddle, it can rust and the handle rot, making it valueless; just as squandered money becomes useless.

If you carefully put your brand-new shovel up in the attic to keep it pristine, occasionally check up on it to make sure it is still shiny, and **keep** it safely there; it is as valueless to both you and your neighbors as though it had never existed.

*A man…called his servants…and to one gave five talents, to another two, and to another one; each according to his…ability.*

*Then he that received the five talents went and traded with them…and likewise he that received two. But he that received one went and digged in the earth, and hid his lord's money.*

*After a long time the lord of those servants reckoned… with them. And so he that had received the five talents came and brought the other five he had earned*

*His Lord said unto him, well done thou good and faithful servant: thou hast been faithful over a few things; I will make* thee a ruler over many things: enter thou into the joy of thy lord.

Likewise, the servant that had been given the two talents showed the additional two he had earned.

Again, His lord said unto him, well done thou good and faithful servant; thou hast been faithful over a few things; I will make thee a ruler over many things: enter thou into the joy of thy lord.

Then he which received the one talent came and said Lord I knew that thou art a hard man, reaping where thou hast not sown, gathering where thou hast not strewed: and I was afraid, and went and hid thy talent in the earth: lo, there thou hast what is thine.

His lord answered and said unto him, Thou wicked and slothful servant, thou knewest that I reap where I sow not, and gather where I have not strewed: thou oughtest therefore to have put my money to the exchangers … and then…I should have received my own with interest.

Then, in the parlance of the day, he said, "You're fired!"[16]

Back to that shovel in the attic.  It the owner had no need of it; he could have lent or rented it to a gardening neighbor.  Because of it, a few seeds could have become an abundance of beauty and food.

A miser's money horde does no one, not even the miser, any good.

# LESSON EIGHT
## The Pinocchio Effect

*The rich ruleth over the poor and the borrower is servant to the lender.*[17]

In ancient times, the final collateral for all debt was a person's own body, and the bodies of everyone else in his household. If you did not pay back a loan; you, your spouse, and all your children became slaves.

Today we do not become literal slaves, but many do become emotional slaves to people, organizations and jobs because their debt load makes changing too dangerous.

Many self-employed individuals willingly make less money in exchange for greater personal control over their daily lives.
Debt eliminates this benefit.

It is obvious we need to pay rent, utilities, wages, taxes and other regular operating expenses before we can determine our net profit. While it can sometimes feel we are a slave to the electric company, at least it doesn't try to tell us how to run our business.
Imagine your favorite relative or closest friend saying, "My son needs a summer job. Can you hire him?" and there is no way you can afford an employee.

You answer, "Not this year."

Now imagine you owe that person money, lots of money.

Hiring the son is still a very bad business decision, but not hiring him could be worse.

Borrowing from a professional lender, a "silent partner," avoids this problem.

Or does it?

Silent partners want to protect their investments.

Because lenders have more money than borrowers, most "silent" partners assume they also have more business acumen. If you were as smart as they, you would be just as rich.

If a "silent partner" disagrees with what you spend on advertising, maintenance, wages, office furniture, research... and you cannot afford to pay him back, you will do things his way.

That can be a very good thing if he truly understands your business better than you do.

If he does not, if he earned his money in a totally different way... You and your investor will both suffer the consequences of his ignorance, but you alone will get the blame should things go south.

Pinocchio started with controlling strings he wanted gone.

Becoming a borrower is living the Pinocchio story backwards.

The lender's golden rule: He who has the gold, pulls the strings and makes the rules.

# LESSON NINE
## Taxes

The benefits of government are a communal debt, and like all debts must be paid.  The only way to honorably avoid payment is to leave, as did the ten tribes when Solomon's son refused to lower taxes.

Taxes are often mentioned in the Bible, including tribute. Tribute is taxation on a conquered people, the benefit being their physical lives.

Like all conquered people, the citizens of Israel under Roman rule hated paying tribute.  Not only was it expensive, but much of the money went to support heathen temples and immoral lifestyles which violated Jewish law.   That made being anti-tax even more popular than it is today, and much more dangerous.

*"Master, we know thou art true, and teach the way of God in truth, neither carest thou for any man; for thou regardest not the person of the man, tell us therefore, what thinkest thou? Is it lawful to give tribute unto Caesar...?"*

*..."Show me the tribute money...Whose is this image and inscription?"*

*"Caesar's"*

*"Render therefore unto Caesar those things which are Caesar's; and unto God the things that are God's"*[18]

We need to be aware of all government obligations, and pay them.

## LESSON TEN
## "And unto God..."

We are told to give to God that which is His, but what is that?

*The earth is the Lord's, and the fullness thereof; the world, and they that dwell therein.*[19]

We are only the caretakers; all abilities and all possessions are gifts on loan from God.

Every breath we take is a divine gift.

When we tithe, we are not "giving" to God. We are merely meeting an obligation to Him by returning a small portion of His gifts.

Our thoughts and the words we express are all we possess, all we can give. God values our gift of words

*...they that feared the Lord spake often one to another... "And they shall be mine," saith the Lord of Hosts...*[20]

It is vital to find something in each day to give thanks for. There will be days of misery. Unless the habit of thankfulness is established from the beginning, it will not be there to nourish us when needed.

When on that "worst of days" you manage to give thanks, you will feel more positive, more confident there is a master plan. A solution exists

It is then easier to be what every entrepreneur must be: a problem solver.

Should there come a day so black it seems you will lose all?

*Naked came I out of my Mother's womb, and naked I shall return thither: the lord gave and the Lord hath taken away; blessed be the name of the Lord.*[21]

When Job spoke the above words, he had not a penny to tithe or strength to help others.
It would be easy to conclude he had nothing to give.
That would be wrong.
Job had not lost his reason—his inspiration—for giving thanks and praise to his redeeming God. He still knew that being thankful and blessing the Lord is both a continuous obligation and a privilege.

The Book of Job should be required reading for every would-be-entrepreneur.
Job was responsible for the well being of his family, his servants, and the many who relied on his charity. When, through no fault of his own, he lost his wealth, he let everyone down.
His failure was not private, but public.
It left not just him, but his many servants penniless.

Like Job, modern business owners walk an economic tightrope that can snap, plummeting the owner into economic ruin.
Like Job, we can still give daily thanks to our Redeemer.

Personal experience:

This book was written and re-written over a ten year period. (I'm slow.) When I first wrote this chapter I thought

I had already experienced tough times, and knew what it took to give thanks when times were bad.

I was wrong.

A few years ago my thyroid stopped working. I felt fine. I gained over sixty pounds in less than a year, slept all the time, and did not pay attention to business.

My family doctor didn't care I felt fine. He insisted I get a check up.

He discovered cancer. (I am now a very healthy cancer survivor.)

Driving a car or running a business, if you are asleep at the wheel, you will wreck. I had been asleep at the wheel for over three years.

The first healthy day I sat down and really studied my books, I realized nothing made sense. I grossed more money that year than I normally did in eighteen months, but every day people called, demanding payments on seriously past due bills. I had no money to pay them.

January 2008, I discovered certain employees had been embezzling because I "made it too easy to steal."

By February that year the recession flattened our local economy.

Deep in debt, income down fifty per cent, I turned to the instant credit of Master Charge, Visa and Discover... Only to learn maxed out cards have MUCH higher rates than unused cards.

I felt like Job surely did when told he had lost all his wealth.

Did I give thanks for a redeeming God?
No.
I whined, "How could this happen to me?"
I pouted, "It's not fair!"
I prayed, "Don't let anyone find out how stupid I was!"

By 'anyone', I meant especially my family and close friends. That's right; I cared more about maintaining a fake image than solving the problem.

The more I thought about how bleak everything had become, the more miserable I became.

Whenever I looked in a mirror, a depressing person stared back. Fewer customers wanted anything to do with me or my business.

The red ink in my checkbook sucked me deeper into the self-pity-whirlpool.

One day I picked up an early draft of this book, reread this chapter. I could hear a patient voice, "You believed those words when you wrote them. Why not now?"

I would like to claim that immediately, like Job, I said, "Blessed be the name of the Lord."

I didn't. Misery had become my mantra, my identity. I reveled in my victim hood.

The patient voice kept nudging me, "Why don't you believe now?"

Finally, I attempted a thankful prayer. At first the only thing (Only? This is a BIG thing, but when you are in crybaby mode it is hard to have intelligent perspective.) I could think of was, "Thank you for dying for me."

Hate to admit it, but discovered myself adding, "But how about some help with the mortgage payments?"

Someone died gruesomely so I could have eternal life, and I was worried about mortgage payments!

Something snapped.

I spent the rest of that evening finding things to give thanks for, starting with my beautiful daughters.

While still recognizing blessings, I fell into a peaceful slumber.

The next day I thought about the bleak looks I saw when grocery shopping, at the gas station, and even on people walking their dogs. I wondered, "Did everyone forget how to smile?"

That evening at our scheduled sales meeting, I announced our new store motto: "We are an Oasis of Happiness!"

It was the beginning of our turn around.

I still have both bad and good days.

Every day I say, "Thank you, Lord."

It gives solaces on bad days and increases a good day's joy.

## PART II

# TOP DOG
# IS
# JUST A DOG

The most important place to start our
business development is
with ourselves.

# LESSON ELEVEN
## To see success, look failure in the eye.

If you strive to accomplish something, it seems perfect, and then it fails; be honest with yourself about the failure. Do not be afraid to start over.

*And it repented the Lord that he had made man...*[22]

The gift of free will creates a world in which God cannot force man to love Him.

In other words, God is subject to spiritual happenings just as we are subject to floods, earthquakes and hurricanes.

God admitted that mankind chose to be violently evil. He sent the Great Flood to correct this failure, because he regretted making man. But Noah, a man who freely chose to love God, He saved.

We will have failures.

Failures contain the seed of success that can be clearly seen only when we are honest with ourselves. By salvaging the lessons of past attempts, we can advance forward.

If even God had to start over, we should not be discouraged when we, too, have to "go back to go."

# LESSON TWELVE
## The Blame Game.

The first time Moses led the tribes of Israel to the edge of the Promised Land, the tribes failed to believe that they could secure their new homeland. Because of this lack of faith, Moses announced they were going to be wondering through the wilderness for another forty years.

A group of the more powerful princes protested,

*"...thou make thyself a prince over us? Moreover thou hast not brought us into a land of milk and honey..."*[23]

Those pretenders-to-power chose to blame Moses and Aaron for all failures. They believed that by denying culpability, the consequences of their disobedience could be avoided.

Moses, the real leader, took personal responsibility for not only his transgressions, but for all the tribes as well.


Personal experience:

I believed the Blame Game could never apply to me, a hard working, "the-buck-stops-here" type owner.

Ha!

Consider the following true story. Names have been changed to protect the innocent.

Me, to a customer, "Don't worry, Mrs. Roberts, the last component for your project finally showed up today. We can finish by tomorrow morning."

Mrs. Roberts snapped, "You better! This is my third trip to pick it up! If it's not finished by tomorrow, I'm going elsewhere!"

Multiple shipping problems had plagued us as we worked on Mrs. Robert's project. We saw the mounting difficulties as reasons for delay; she saw them as excuses.

I went to John, an employee, and, *without asking about his current work schedule,* told him "We absolutely must have Mrs. Robert's work done tomorrow morning! Finish it."

John had already promised three other customers he would complete their "quick and easy" projects before closing. Being inexperienced, and therefore sure nothing could go wrong, John never volunteered how full his schedule already was. He "knew" there would be plenty of time to finish Mrs. Robert's project.

I, the experienced one, not only failed to ask, "What else are you working on today?" but worse I never once checked on his progress.

Murphy raised his ugly head.[24]

John struggled so hard to finish the work he had personally promised, he totally forgot about Mrs. Robert.

Mrs. Robert arrived early the next morning. Her project had not even been started.

Me, "I'm so sorry. John said he would finish it immediately. It is so hard to find good help these days!"

Whoops!
Blame Game Guilty!

# LESSON THIRTEEN
## Doing Extra is Business as Usual

*"Oh Lord God of my master Abraham, I pray thee show me good speed this day...let it come to pass, that the damsel to whom I say Let down thy pitcher, I pray thee, that I may drink; and she shall say, drink, and I will give thy camels drink also"* [25]

The eldest and most trusted servant of Abraham was given an important, difficult task: return to the city of Abraham's birth to find a suitable wife for his son and sole heir, Isaac. The servant devised a test to help him select a woman of character.

When Rebecca was asked to share a drink of water, she noticed that the thirsty man was a traveler. If he was thirsty, his animals were surely just as thirsty. Drawing enough water for ten camels would be hard work, but she volunteered her labor because of the obvious need.

This revealed character.

As a result she became Isaac's wife (The ancient equivalent of marrying a handsome young billionaire).

If the children of Isaac were to survive and prosper, they would need to be willing to do more than just the bare minimum. Rebecca proved that she would be a living example of such an attitude.

All business is simply finding a need others have, and getting paid for filling that need. A business person becomes more valuable when, like Rebecca, he gives more than asked for, and does so with a willing heart.


Personal Experience:

I needed a new pair of prescription glasses.

As usual, when asked which style frame I wanted, I said, "Point me to your clearance rack."

The clerk waved to the far corner. "Over there. Come get me when you've picked one." He walked away.

No other customers were waiting to be helped.

After trying on many pairs, I finally found an inexpensive pair that didn't seem too bad.

Since the man who first helped me was now busy, I told another clerk I had picked out a frame and needed fitting.

She sat down at the fitting table. I mentioned I wished I had a second opinion for how the frames looked on me.

She looked closely, said, "Hmmm, I think those are a bit too harsh for your face." First checking their price tag, she left.

She returned with three pair within $15.00 of the same price. "Let's try these."

As I tried the first pair, she showed how the frames accentuated my natural brow line and its colors softened my face, minimizing facial wrinkles.

I happily paid more than first planned.

As I paid my bill, I noticed the man who first "helped" me was spending considerable time with a woman looking at expensive designer frames.

I later learned the lady who helped me with my inexpensive purchase sells more, both in number of frames and total dollar volume, than anyone else in that shop.

Not surprised.

Like Rebecca, she did more than necessary and did so with a willing heart.

# LESSON FOURTEEN
## Pleasure Today, or Treasure Tomorrow?

Expediency: Selfishly acting in the moment, rather than doing what is right and wisest for the long haul.

*...Esau said to Jacob, "Feed me..." And Jacob said, "Sell me thy birthright."*
*..."what profit shall this birthright do to me?"*[26]

For a quick, easy solution to his hunger, Esau gave up his birthright, a future benefit, to his brother Jacob. If instead Jacob had offered to trade the soup for Esau's promise to immediately become a slave, it is doubtful Esau would have taken him up on the offer.

It is often painful to deny ourselves for a benefit it seems we will never live long enough to enjoy. It is tempting to spend money on "necessary" personal luxuries when we should be developing the business first.

*Prepare thy work without, and make it fit for thyself in the field* (business first) *and afterward build thy house.* [27]

After your harvest (profit), you will be free to enjoy a nice home, a fancier car, any good extra that can make your life more fun.

There is another, more insidious, way we make life short-term easy and long-term hard. When we "go along to get along", or trivialize harm by saying, "You have to break eggs to make an omelet." or worse yet abandon sacred beliefs because "principles are of no value," we are sacrificing our spiritual birthright.

In this world we risk losing our personal reputation; in the next world we jeopardize much more.

*For what is a man profited, if he shall gain the whole world, and lose his own soul?*[28]

Faith in God makes it easier to forfeit a shallow pleasure today so that tomorrow might be better.

"Easier," unfortunately, isn't the same as "easy."

# LESSON FIFTEEN
## Use someone else's 20-20 hind sight!

*Honor thy father and thy mother that thy days may be long on the land which the lord thy God hath given thee.*[29]

*Thou shalt rise up...and honour the face of the old man, and fear thy God...*[30]

In the brutal world of three thousand years ago, the cost of ignorance was death.  People who listened to their experienced elders lived longer and better.

Today, we have libraries of history books to help us learn from our elders.

We may have new gadgets in our lives, but the emotions that govern our lives have not changed. *There is nothing new under the sun.*[31] Those who learn from history have 20-20 vision in a world of the nearsighted.  To not listen to the voice of experience is like putting on a blindfold before going on a walk.

Not all advice is created equal. How can one recognize wise advice?

There are clues.  For instance:

*...a flattering mouth worketh ruin.*[32]

These words are attributed to Solomon by the men of Hezekiah.

Solomon's own son Rehoboam chose to ignore that advice.

Solomon had taxed the people heavily to build his magnificent temple. After Solomon's death, *all Israel came and spake to Rehoboam,*[33] asking to have the "temporary" temple-building taxes eliminated.

All the old men who had served with his father advised Rehoboam *to be kind* (lower the taxes).[34]

The sycophantic young men appealed to Rehoboam's vanity. They advised him to be more demanding than his father had been. (You can almost hear them saying, "You're the man!")

Rehoboam foolishly followed *the advice of the young men,*[35] and immediately lost most of his kingdom when ten of the twelve tribes refused to pay any more taxes.[36]

Not everyone will lose over two-thirds of their business should they choose to ignore experienced advice, but considering how many people say "if I knew then what I know now" the loss in time and money is enormous.

A person who consistently gives good advice is a treasure.

# LESSON SIXTEEN
## Real Men say Thank You!

To avoid his brother's wrath, and to seek a wife, Jacob fled to his Uncle Laban's territory.

Laban welcomed his nephew to his home.

Jacob said 'Thank you' to his uncle not with words, but with action. He pitched in and helped his uncle.

In only a month Laban knew that Jacob was the type of hard working man he wanted around permanently. Obviously such a skilled, hardworking employee would not settle for working for only room and board.

Laban asked Jacob *"what shall thy wages be?"*

*"...I will serve thee seven years for Rachel thy younger daughter."*

Laban readily agreed. *And Jacob served seven years for Rachel...*[37]

With the benefit of Jacob's labor, Laban's fortunes grew. He should have been thankful.

Instead he suddenly decided it "wasn't right" that the younger daughter should marry before the older daughter, and tricked Jacob into marrying the older one. As if that weren't enough, Jacob had to work yet another seven years for the bride he loved.

Each time he swindled Jacob, Laban became richer—at that moment.

When it came time for Jacob to return to the Promised Land, he told his wives

"*...with all my power I have served your father.  And your father has deceived me, and changed my wages ten times...*"[38]

Jacob announced it was time for him to leave with all he had been promised.

Neither he nor his wives believed Laban would willingly give up Jacob's profitable labor. If Jacob were to return home, it would have to be without Laban's knowledge.

Jacob would not be able to leave without the willing cooperation of both wives.

Their response?

"*Is there yet any portion or inheritance for us in our father's house? Are we not counted as strangers?  For he hath sold us, and hath quite devoured also our money.*" [39]

They, their servants and children all helped Jacob sneak away.

People who feel cheated too often justify "cheating back."

It isn't just polite; it is good business to be appreciative when helped by others.

# LESSON SEVENTEEN
## Losers VS Superstars

When Jacob realized he had been tricked by Laban, he could easily have stopped being a good and faithful servant. He didn't.

Instead Jacob continued to do the best job he could for his conniving father-in-law. Because of Jacob's efforts, the undeserving Laban became richer.

Even though Laban cheated Jacob out of an extra seven years and *changed his wages ten times* (obviously **not** by giving him a raise), Laban could not cheat Jacob out of the skills and mental habits developed by striving to do your best.

Such a mind set is of greater value than gold.

Laban, less capable on his own, fades into a mere footnote of history.

Jacob had arrived at Laban's home with only the clothes on his back. He left wealthy.

Of greater value than the flocks he earned were the well-honed skills and knowledge Jacob developed while working for Laban. This expertise enabled Jacob to continue to generate even more wealth.

If Jacob had used Laban's behavior to rationalize working slovenly, he would surely have become habituated to being a slacker.

Working less, Jacob would have learned less; thus cheating himself.

Losers rationalize cheating back.

Super stars play their best even when on a losing team.

# LESSON EIGHTEEN
## Fear Goggles

When I was in college friends joked about "beer goggles", how the world looked after one beer too many.

Fear is more distorting.

When Jacob/Israel returned home he feared being killed by his twin brother Esau. The birthright he had stolen from Esau was worth more than any wealth mortal man could create. When Jacob stole it, he cheated Esau more than Laban had ever cheated him.

Would Esau still want to kill him? Jacob believed, "Yes!"

Every piece of information Jacob learned about his estranged brother he filtered through his guilt-driven fear, blinding him to the changes twenty years had wrought.

Esau had stayed home; obtained brides on his own terms; developed herds and wealth for himself, not a greedy father-in-law. Like Frank Sinatra, he could sing "and more, much more this, I did it my way."

It didn't bother Esau that his way was not God's way, he cared only for the wealth he had so successfully accumulated.

All this Jacob could have learned by simply sending a messenger to his brother. Instead Jacob fearfully sent spies who returned with incomplete information.[40]

When Esau greeted him with love and tears not hate and spears, you can feel Jacob's shocked relief. (That "gifts" were sufficient payment for Esau's fighting men, not total plunder, was also undoubtedly an equal relief.)

When we carry a burden of unforgiven guilt, we anticipate punishment.

If this punishment does not come from the outside, we will create it ourselves, just as Jacob sent the best of his flocks ahead to his brother in an attempt to bribe forgiveness.

Anything that generates intense feelings of guilt should be honestly dealt with before you let it sabotage your life.

*The wicked flee where no man pursueth: the righteous are as bold as a lion.*[41]

Faith in God's infinite ability to forgive not only assures us of the opportunity to live with Him forever, it also frees our spirit to fully develop the talents He has blessed us with here on earth.

# LESSON NINETEEN
## Bribing God

People who can be bribed are available to the highest bidder.

If someone asked if God could be bribed; if He, too, could be available to the highest bidder, most of us would be shocked, offended and perhaps even angered. We would shout "No!"

At first glance this seems so obvious. What is the grandest cathedral compared to the plainest mountain? What do we possess that is not part of God's creation? "Do not try to bribe God." would seem not worth mentioning.

But "fox-hole-promises" are as common in the business world as they are on the battlefield. "God just let me live through this and I will..." is a common prayer.

If what is being offered is a thing of this world, it implies that the petitioner believes he has more power than God over that object. Yet the Creator of heaven and earth already possesses all of his creation. We are simply caretakers. All we can offer Him are things of our heart, spirit and soul.

Three hundred years after the Israelites had taken possession of the Promised Land, a king of Ammon decided to take back some of the conquered territory.

The Israelis elders picked *Jephthah...a mighty man of valor* to lead them into battle.

Jephthah's first official action was to send *messengers unto the king of the children of Ammon saying What hast thou to do with me, that thou art come against me to fight in our land?*[42]

The King replied that because his ancestors had once owned the land, Israel should give it back.

Jephthah responded with a detailed history of how Israel acquired the disputed territory. Jephthah quoted from the scriptures we know as Deuteronomy.

Jephthah concluded with

*...the Lord the Judge be judge this day between the children of Israel and the children of Ammon...And Jephthah vowed a vow unto the Lord and said If Thou shalt without fail deliver the children of Ammon into my hands, then it shall be that whatsoever cometh forth of the doors of my house to meet me, when I return in peace from the children of Ammon, shall surely be the Lord's, and I will offer it up for a burnt offering.*[43]

Jephthah had already stated that God would judge. He could have said he would give thanks after the victory, but to offer to sacrifice not **WHEN** but **IF** he won implied that God was available to the highest bidder.

*The Lord delivered the children of Ammon into his hands... and Jephthah came...to his house, and...his daughter came out to meet him with timbrels and with dances: and she was his only child...when he saw her, he rent his clothes and said "Alas my daughter! Thou hast brought me very low, and thou art one of them that trouble me: for I have opened my mouth unto the Lord and I cannot go back.*

*And she said unto him, "My father, if thou hast opened up thy mouth unto the Lord, do to me according to that which hath proceeded out of thy mouth..."*[44]

After two months with her friends she was sacrificed. She would have been taught by her father that obedience to God could not be compromised.

Her father, though, had proved he was very familiar with the scriptures describing the early days of conquest. He would surely have been familiar with the reasons there were whole peoples God wanted obliterated, words that appeared just after those terrifying commands.

*...for abomination to the Lord, which He Hateth, have they done unto their gods; for even their sons and their daughters they have burnt in the fire to their gods.*[45]

The apparent request to sacrifice his daughter was an evil one, resulting from a pagan belief system, and a pagan practice.

The Israelites were surrounded by people who believed in capricious gods, gods who had to be continuously bribed. God had warned his people about the dangerous attraction of other ways.

Evil actions eventually have evil results, unless the evil is acknowledged and divine forgiveness sought.

God forgave Aaron for creating and worshipping a golden calf. He could just as easily have forgiven Jephthah for both ignoring the strict laws regarding sacrifice and his rash implication that God the Judge would not judge fairly, but instead could be swayed by a bribe.

He sacrificed his daughter not because of his faith, but because of his lack of faith in a just God.

What does this have to do with us? Too often we make the same mistake.

Even the most loving parent cannot be with his child every minute of his life. Parents leave to fight wars, build bridges, negotiate contracts, and many other necessary activities.

Sometimes the loving parent, lacking faith in God's promise of an abundant life, is absent longer than necessary.

When that happens, the child is sacrificed to the unforgiving fires of time.

# LESSON TWENTY
## Desires Sire Deeds

*Thou shalt not covet thy neighbor's house; thou shalt not covet thy neighbor's wife, nor his manservant, nor his maid servant, nor his ox, nor his ass, nor anything that is thy neighbor's.*[46]

*...the desire of the righteous shall be granted.*[47]
*The desire of the righteous is only good.*[48]

Our true inner thoughts define what we are and who we will become; *for as he thinketh in his heart, so is he.*[49]

America was founded by immigrants who, like Abraham, left their known homes for the unknown so that their descendents might live better lives.

This same desire has inspired many to leave the known "safety" of employment for the unpredictable world of self-employment.

An economically abundant life is as much a motivation for today's business person as having large herds was for Abraham.

This desire inspires us to create so much value that someone will pay for our labor. We create value by digging ditches; painting pictures; inventing better mouse traps; even providing entertainment.

As much as the desire to earn a better lifestyle can help us, being consumed with the desire to possess someone else's home, bank account, car, or spouse will hurt us.

**Coveting focuses not on what we can create, but on what we can take.**

When coveting makes someone steal an elderly man's social security checks, its evil is obvious.

What if you are hired to do a job, but leave out a small part because "everyone else skips it too?" The customer isn't getting all he has paid for, but suffers no harm. If the customer isn't "really" hurt, is that theft?

Or have you rationalized coveting into invisibility?

Rationalized coveting creates shortsighted greed.

Any action, even if legal, that creates immediate monetary gain at the unwilling expense of another—-inferior repair parts, creative accounting, enhanced billing hours, false advertising, betrayal—is theft.

Theft means more wealth today.

Thieves with both guns and fountain pens can readily see today's gain.

It is hard to see what is not there, the future wealth that could have been.

The book *The Loyalty Effect* compared numerous "nice-guy" businesses with their more common worldly-wise counter parts.

In every industry, the nice-guy companies were at some point berated by their peers for not doing obvious, but slightly dishonorable, actions that would have improved the immediate bottom line.

In every case the nice-guy companies not only eventually did better than their "more commonsensical" peers, but in many cases thrived while the "wiser" competitor went bankrupt.

The nice guys were the last ones left standing.

Can we tell if we have crossed the line from good desire to destructive coveting?

*...where envying and strife is, there is confusion...but the wisdom that is from above is full of good fruits...and without hypocrisy.*[50]

God took chaos and created a universe.
We recognize needs and create businesses.
Our desires, what we most want, will determine the direction of those businesses.

*...seek ye first the kingdom of God.*[51]
*Commit thy works unto the Lord, and thy thoughts shall be established.*[52]

It is our choice.  We can let God, the Ultimate Creator, define our desires, or we can limit ourselves to our own ideas.

# PART III

Onward into the World!

# BUSYNESS

# TO

# TO BUSINESS

# LESSON TWENTY-ONE
# POWER!

Pharaoh was deeply troubled by two dreams he knew had meaning.

First seven fat cows were devoured by seven skeletal cows.

Then seven fat ears of corn were consumed by seven withered ears.

He knew these dreams were divine messages, but of what? What should he do?

Joseph, inspired by God, interpreted the dreams as being seven years of exceptional plenty, followed by seven years of the worst famine Egypt had ever seen. He then offered a plan for Pharaoh to both personally prosper and to save Egypt.

Pharaoh listened, believed and acted.

*Pharaoh said unto Joseph...See I have set thee over all the land of Egypt.*[53]

Joseph implemented God's plan.

Without the knowledge provided by Joseph, Pharaoh would have been under the illusion he had power while he was busily doing his daily actions, but in reality he would have been just as weak as anyone when the famine hit.

If after Joseph had interpreted his dreams, Pharaoh had chosen to do nothing, the seven years of famine would have left him powerless.

Only when the knowledge of what to do was combined with action, did Pharaoh become truly powerful.

# LESSON TWENTY-TWO
## Delegation is Multiplication

"If I want something done right, I have to do it myself."
"If I don't do it, nobody will."
"Why can't anybody else get it right?"

The more we say the above, the more we will believe them. The more we believe them, the more they will be true.

It is tempting to believe that if we are the "only one who can get it right", we must be more important.

Can you imagine, on hearing Joseph's plan to survive the coming famine, Pharaoh saying, "Get my chariot, I'm going out to buy grain. This is too important to leave to anyone else."

Pharaohs were trained from birth to regard competent servants as extenuations of themselves. A servant's accomplishments did not diminish a pharaoh, they enhanced him. They also freed him from being a slave to all the "have-to-do's" of daily life.

Giving all the management power to Joseph made Pharaoh more, not less, powerful.

It is important to note that Joseph also delegated power. His plan included middle level management.

Most of us have not been trained from birth to manage others. Either we did our tasks, or they didn't get done. As long as we have few responsibilities, that is fine. But as your business becomes successful, it will become more complicated.

From the time Moses met his wife until he was sent back to Egypt, he was responsible for only a small group of people. Leaving Egypt, he became the leader of over a million.

While Moses was leading the Chosen People through the wilderness, Jethro, his successful father-in-law, visited him.

Moses complained he couldn't get to the business of leading because of all the many petty, time-wasting squabbles people expected him to resolve.

Jethro explained:

*The thing thou doest is not good. Thou shalt surely wear away, both thou **and this people with thee;** thou art not able to perform it thy self alone...I will counsel thee... provide out of all the people able men...to be rulers of thousands...hundreds...tens...every great matter they shall bring to thee, but every small matter they shall judge: so it shall be easier for thyself, and they shall bear the burden with thee. If thou shalt do this thing...then thou shalt be able to endure...[54]*

By giving up power to others, by acknowledging that he was not the only capable judge, Moses became a more effective leader.

But, he did give up some of his power.

Does giving up power make us less?

When Jesus visited Capernaum, the elders of the city asked him to come heal the dying servant of a local centurion. Jesus agreed, and went with them towards the centurion's home.

*...the centurion sent friends to him, saying...Lord...I am not worthy that thou shouldest enter under my roof...but say in a word, and my servant shall be healed. For I also am a man set under authority, having under me soldiers, and I say unto one, Go, and he goeth; and to another, Come and he cometh; and to my servant, Do this, and he doeth it....*

*And they that were sent returned to the (centurion's) house, found the servant whole that had been sick.*[55]

As an army officer, the centurion understood that since Christ was more powerful than an ordinary man, He therefore had more authority to delegate.

# LESSON TWENTY-THREE
## A Human Crutch: To use or to be?

God commanded Moses to go deliver a message to Pharaoh. Moses pointed out to God that when it came to talking, he was effectively a "verbal cripple."

> ...And Moses said I am slow of speech... The Lord said... Is not Aaron the Levite thy brother? I know he can speak well... he shall be...thy spokesman ...and thou shalt be to him instead of God.[56]

In other words, God would deliver the message to Moses, who would deliver it to Aaron, who would deliver it to the people.

In the famous movie <u>The Ten Commandments,</u> Charlton Hesston should have played Aaron, not Moses.

Moses alone was incomplete; he needed Aaron's oratorical strength.

At first glance, this looks like delegation, but it is more than that. When you delegate you assign someone to do what, if you had the time, you could eventually do.

This is different. God assigned Moses a seemingly impossible task: public speaking.

When Moses attempted to use his speech problems to avoid God's calling, *the anger of the Lord was kindled against him.*[57]

Why?

Because Moses should have had faith a way would be found. Utilizing the natural resources the Lord provides includes using the talents of others.

That Moses needed Aaron's help is obvious. That Aaron needed Moses' help even more is not as obvious.

Aaron, a devout Israelite, desired to do God's will, but he lacked the ability to hear God.

Aaron was as dependent on Moses as Moses was on him.

# LESSON TWENTY-FOUR
## Be trustworthy

*...thou shalt love thy neighbor as thyself.*[58]

Every business consists of taking something, finding a way to add value to it, and selling it to someone else.

The "something" can be our own labor (like a lawyer), someone else's labor (example: a cleaning franchise), things (including silly things, like pet rocks) or a combination (for instance, a night's lodging in a motel).

Every business that survives sells their product for more than it costs to create it; that is called a profit.

If you are selling something which, if in the same circumstance as your customer, you would want someone to sell to you, you are showing love.

Honest selling follows the golden rule.

If, on the other hand, you would never buy what you are selling because you believe it has no positive value, you are not being trustworthy. You are running a con game.

Whether your con game is legal or illegal is irrelevant.

Whether others perceive it as moral or immoral is irrelevant.

You know in your heart if buying it yourself is an expression of self-love or self-abuse.

Note: Order taking isn't selling. Your customer has the freedom to disregard your advice. Unless you believe harm could result, you have as much right as anyone to profit from any legal buying decision.

# LESSON TWENTY-FIVE
# Do not be too trusting

*Now there arose a new king over Egypt, which knew not Joseph.*[59]

A man's word, no matter how powerful or how well intended, is limited to his lifetime and to the forces he is capable of controlling.

When the Israelites went from being honored guests to *'lives bitter with bondage'*[60], anyone protesting "We had an agreement!" would have been treated more scornfully than modern workers protesting to new corporate owners about the loss of promised pensions.

Given the choice between trusting mortal man and trusting eternal God, the choice should be obvious.
It is not always easy to tell if such a choice is being made.


Personal Experience:

From the first time I interviewed my new bookkeeper, to her second to the last day on the job; her poise, dress and professional skills intimidated me.

It took me over two hours to balance the business checkbook. She did it accurately in less than a half hour.

Her predecessor spent half the day filing the previous day's paperwork. The new girl had it finished before her morning coffee break.

I soon learned it was best to just get out of her way and let the professional do her job—not easy since we shared a small office.

There were things that bothered me, which I asked her to do differently.

Me: "The last bookkeeper always paper-clipped the check that I was to sign to the bill it paid. I liked that."

Her: "That's so inefficient! You have so little office time. It's easier if I just print up the checks first thing in the morning and have you sign them before you get busy. You shouldn't waste your time hanging out in the office while I pull invoices."

Me: "OK."

One afternoon I walked into an unexpectedly re-arranged office.

Me: "Why is your desk in the middle of the room? It looks like its pinning you into the corner! Doesn't working in such a small space feel claustrophobic?"

Her: "People are always coming and going, talking to you about this and that; it is so distractive! I will be able to work much more efficiently with this arrangement."

Me: "OK."

She was the professional. I was merely an untrained former door to door salesman who had managed to morph into a business owner.

I could have demanded she do things my way, but catering to her preferences seemed a small price to pay to keep her happy.

I did have the skills and knowledge to check the accuracy of her work. After the first month I chose not to.

Why should I? The few times I did, she had zero errors! I concentrated on the fun parts of my business: product research, talking with customers, planning...

When the Israelites went from honored guest to slaves, was it a sudden change? Were there warning signs they should have heeded? Had the Israelites grown complacent, too lazy to anticipate future problems?

We do not know.

I do know I became lazy.

I told myself I was being trusting.

At Income tax time, I took my books to the accountant. She said, "Your credit card records are a mess!"

Every irritating quirk of my bookkeeper flashed through my mind. "I'll look into it tonight."

That night, as soon as everyone left, I reviewed each returned check from the previous year, comparing every entry—all four thousand plus—with what the computer history said it was.

I found altered checks, forged signatures, totally misentered checks, utility bills and credit card payments with **her** account numbers...

I had not realized there were motives behind my bookkeeper's actions. Not attaching checks to bills made it easy for payments to be misapplied. Her desk rearrangement made it impossible to easily observe her work.

The money taken is gone.

For the next seven years I became a slave to the economic consequences of my "trusting" laziness.

# LESSON TWENTY-SIX
## Humble all the way to the bank

When Joseph's family came to Egypt, it wasn't just his twelve brothers and father; it was the whole tribe; their wives, many children, servants, huge flocks and herds.

It would have seemed like a small invasion.

When the citizens of Egypt were starving, to see that many strangers and animals given the best, could have bred resentment. Even "divine" pharaohs were known to meet untimely deaths if they became too unpopular.

Joseph wisely forestalled such resentment before it started.

*...When Pharaoh shall say...What is your occupation? That ye shall say ...cattle...for every shepherd is an abomination unto the Egyptians.*[61]

How could lowly shepherds be worth an Egyptian's notice? How fortunate Joseph's family could take over a necessary but disdainful occupation, freeing the Egyptians from dirtying their hands.

There can be great profit in activities others consider beneath them.

Personal Experience:

While buffing a marble floor in a bank, a friend of mine watched a mother walk in with her teenage son.

She pointed at my friend and said, "That is why you must study hard. You don't want to end up like him."

What she didn't know is that my friend had put himself through college cleaning homes. His family expected him to get a "real job" after he graduated. Instead, he expanded his cleaning business.

Today, he has dozens of employees and makes more money than the president of that bank.

His willingness to get a little honest dirt under his fingernails lets him add a great deal of honest green to his bank account.

# LESSON TWENTY-SEVEN
## If you can't say anything nice...

*Thou shalt not go up and down as a talebearer....thou shalt love they neighbor as thyself...*[62]

Just in case we are tempted to think that such rules apply only to our friendly neighbors, earlier Moses admonishes us *Thou shalt not raise a false report...*just a few sentences later adds *if thou meet thy enemy's ox...going astray...bring it back to him again.*[63]

Speech is more than words. "Speaking negatively about the competition" includes taking joy from his suffering. *Rejoice not when thy enemy falleth, and let not thine heart be glad when he stumbleth...*[64]

All gossip distorts the truth. It can hurt the person talked about. It will hurt us taletellers as well.

When I say something negative about another person or his business, it reinforces those beliefs in my mind, making it harder to see his positive attributes.

In business, as in war, it is important to see your adversary accurately.

In today's modern world of mergers and acquisitions, we never know when yesterday's competition could become today's business partner.

Today's verbally sown seeds of ill-will can poison tomorrow's opportunities.

81

# LESSON TWENTY-EIGHT
## Venture Vision

*And the lord Spake unto Moses saying, send thou men that they may search the land of Canaan...And Moses sent them to spy out the land of Canaan...they returned from searching of the land after forty days...and said We came unto the land whither thou sent us, and surely it floweth with milk and honey...Never the less, the people be strong that dwell in the land...Caleb stilled the people...and said Let us go up at once and possess it.*

*But the men that went up with him said, we be not able to go up against the people for they are stronger than we. And they brought up an evil report of the land...*[65]

When thinking about attacking a new market, or researching the desirability of a new product, we should scout the terrain in advance.

It is important to remember that all collected data is useless, until it is interpreted. Market research is no better than the spirit of the market researcher.

Those who are too easily intimidated by the competition will always find reasons to delay entering new products, opening new branches or even starting a new business.

As every entrepreneur knows, **only those who have enough faith to take a chance are worthy of the Promised Land.**

# LESSON TWENTY-NINE
## Backstabbers and Knives

Gideon was a war hero!

Against all odds, he had defeated the Midianites, ensuring (for the moment) Israel's independence.

If Gideon could do so well in war, wouldn't Israel do better if he did all the thinking for them in times of peace as well? Israel's leaders came to him, saying:

*"Rule thou over us, both thou and thy son, and thy son's son also..."*[66]

Gideon replied *"I will not rule over you, neither shall my son rule over you; the Lord shall rule over you"* [67]

After wisely making sure he was well paid for his soldiering, Gideon went home to his seventy sons and many wives.

When Gideon died, one of his sons, Abimelech, decided that the old man was wrong to turn down a kingship. By himself, he could do nothing about such unfairness, but he sought allies.

Abimelech went *unto his mother's brethren* threatening them with the image of his seventy brothers reigning over them, or just one person—himself.

He concluded with *remember also I am your bone and your flesh.*[68] As was the custom of the day, if Abimelech were to become king, they would share in the goodies.

Their greed freed their wallets. Abimelech's relatives hired a small band of mercenary thugs to kill all seventy of his brothers. All but the youngest, who had hidden, were executed.

At first Abimelech and his relatives enjoyed their new wealth and power. Unfortunately, they had all learned that the easiest path to wealth was through treachery.

The country had enjoyed forty peaceful years under Gideon's influence. After only three years of Abimelech's rule, treachery became standard.

Mistrust and paranoia led to the violent deaths of Abimelech and all of his accomplices.[69]

In a modern business setting, backstabbing more commonly results in the green flow of dollars rather than the red flow of blood, but the emotions are the same.

Some businesses encourage different sub-entities to see themselves as in competition with each other more than in competition with other companies.

The musical comedy How to Succeed in Business Without Really Trying is about a young man who goes to work for such a firm. Early in the movie there is a scene in which numerous executives are in a restroom, each obviously worried about the young star as well as each other. They sing a song whose main refrain is "I've got to get that man before he gets me."

As the show develops, the protagonist "wins" the promotion competition by trickery rather than accomplishment. He becomes the new head of the company.

For him it was a happily-ever-after ending.

The movie was popular, and is still fun to see. But how do businesses like that function in the real world?

Would an executive be so busy worrying about the person down the hall, that he would ignore the rival business down the block?

Would the continuous infighting make loss of market share or product obsolescence a shock?

If the movie were about a real business, its happy ending would be an unhappy ending for the shareholders and other employees.

Just like Abimelech was murdered by his accomplices, people who seek your help to betray another, will be just as willing to deceive you.

# LESSON THIRTY
# Family as Foundation

*"It is not good that man should be alone."*[70]

We need a personal, loving support, not just business net working. God declared that Adam **needed** Eve.

The more important something is, the more important it is that it has a good foundation.

The relationship between a man and his wife is so important that God ordered:

*When a man hath taken up a new wife, he shall not go to war, neither shall he be charged with any business: but he shall be free at home one year, and shall cheer up his wife which he hath taken.*[71]

The social support we have from our families come from the generations both before and after us; and from the wife to the husband and the husband to the wife.

For both good and evil, our choices affect those we live with. Each choice has the potential of supporting or discouraging a loved one.

*He that troubleth his own house shall inherit the wind...*[72]

The most important job in the Bible is preserving and spreading the Word of God. Family life is an integral part of it *for if a man know not how to rule his own house, how shall he take care of the Church of God?*[73]

If we choose to neglect our own families, why should anyone trust us to care about an employee?

**PART IV**

# THE MORE WE GROW, THE MORE WE NEED OTHERS.

# LESSON THIRTY-ONE
## Having and Being a Worthy Mate

There is an old story about a young Iroquois girl who saved her tribe.

Her grandmother was the guardian of the seed corn during the winter so that there would be enough for the tribe to plant the next year.

One year the winter was exceptionally long and harsh. No game could be found; the stored food was almost gone. The famished people stormed the young girl's lodge, brutally forced her grandmother aside and gathered up all the seed corn for a great feast.

Fortunately, the young girl had seen them coming, and hid some of the seed corn before it could be squandered.

Only a few days later the warmth of spring finally returned to the Iroquois village. All the tribe were both ashamed and fearful because there was no corn to plant. The elders knew the one forbidden feast was surely going to cause starvation the next winter.

The young girl then surprised her elders with the hidden seed.

She was honored for having more willpower than all the tribal elders because even though she also starved, she knew and acted on the knowledge that the one meal would cost many meals the next year.

There are many other examples, both ancient and modern, of delayed gratification making the difference between solvency and bankruptcy:

> A shepherd who eats like a vegetarian because he is building up his herd.

> The business owner who foregoes a new car so he can buy new sales stock.

> The frugal mother who mends an outfit rather than buy new.

Our own will power is essential. Esau's lack of will power cost him his birthright.

Unfortunately, it doesn't make a bit of difference how much will power you have, if your spouse flagrantly spends what should be your "financial seed corn."

Is there a way to tell in advance if a prospective mate is the type to indulge with the "seed corn?"

Yes.

God created us to take delight in our spouse. As with all the rest of His earthly creation, we are driven to do so. A *person who can distinguish between a time to embrace and a time to refrain from embracing*[74], and to faithfully act on that knowledge, is both wise and virtuous.

If a virtuous woman has extra money, she doesn't squander it. Instead she actively looks for ways to increase its value; such as buying and improving real estate (*she considereth a field, and buyeth it...she planteth a vineyard...*) or other business endeavors (*she maketh fine linen and selleth it..*). Such a spouse adds to her family's wealth. She indeed has a value *far above rubies.*[75]

This is more than a beautiful figure of speech. It is a simple statement of fact.

On the other hand, a spouse who enters a marriage with wealth, but no self-restraint, can quickly use up any financial reserve. As the old saying goes, the quickest way to create a small fortune is to inherit a large one.

When Thomas Stanley did his research for <u>The Millionaire Next Door</u> and its sequel <u>The Millionaire Mind</u>, the one thing he found to be the most common indicator of financial success was marital stability and fidelity. Those who were unfaithful were always less successful than they otherwise would have been!

God wants his people to prosper.

He wants each of us to have, and be, a mate who will help create a successful, abundant union.

He wants us to have, and be, a mate capable of exercising delayed gratification.

It is not to deny us pleasure that he orders *Thou shalt not commit adultery.*[76]

# LESSON THIRTY-TWO
## Loyalty is a three legged stool.

Loyalty, the most important virtue to look for in either a business partner or a spouse, cannot exist unless supported by charity, thankfulness and self-sacrifice.

If a person is incapable of short-term sacrifice, he will be even more incapable of the long-range sacrifices necessary for a true partnership.

If he cannot both graciously receive charity, and with joyful thankfulness share with others, he will find it difficult to participate in the cycles of give and take that constitute any long-term partnership.

Before David son of Jessie was king, he was a fugitive fleeing from King Saul's murderous rage.

Saul had the power to grant wealth and favors to whomever he chose; David could offer only a mercenary's perilous life.

Given the choice between the luxury of being in the king's inner circle and the hardships of hiding in caves, David's men chose the caves.

They had more faith in David's loyalty than Saul's fickleness.

David stayed loyal to his jealous king. The strength of that loyalty was tested every time he could easily have killed Saul.

What gave David the power to practice and inspire such selfless loyalty?

Heredity surely had a part in it. His Great-Grandmother was Ruth, daughter-in-law of Naomi.

The Book of Ruth is the story of loyalty. Loyalty of people to each other and loyalty to God even when it seems He has *dealt very bitterly against us.*

When we first meet Ruth, she delivers her beautiful speech to Naomi:

*Entreat me not to leave thee, or to return from following after thee: for whither thou goest, I will go; and where thou lodgest, I will lodge: thy people shall be my people, and thy God my God: Where thou diest, will I die, and there will I be buried: The Lord do so to me, and more also, if ought but death part thee and me.*

At this point we do not yet know if her pleading is inspired by her love for her mother-in-law, or if—unlike Naomi's other daughter-in-law, Orpah— Ruth has no other place to go and wisely fears being alone in a very dangerous world.

The two grieving widows traveled to Bethlehem together.

As soon as Naomi and Ruth had a place to stay, Ruth took on hard menial labor, gleaning fields, to help support them. The first field she went to belonged to Boaz, a man who followed the law of Moses by allowing *the poor and the stranger*[77] to share the harvest.

When Boaz showed up to inspect the harvest, his first comment wasn't about work, it was *"The Lord be with you."* When Boaz spotted the new girl, he immediately asked his overseer to tell him more about her.

The ancient world had no government safety nets. Each harvest determined not just wealth but survival. If Boaz allowed someone else to manage the harvest, it meant there was strong trust between them.

The overseer's reply would include the details his master would most want to know.

In a business-like fashion the overseer first identified who Ruth was and how she asked permission to glean. The overseer then added *so she came, and hath continued even from morning until now.*

In other words, Ruth worked hard not just in the cool morning when it was easy, but even in the heat of the day when most would take a needed break.

Boaz told Ruth to stay with his maidens under the watchful protection of his men. (Gleaning fields was not just hard, thirsty work, but also exposed the defenseless to physical abuse and sexual predators.)

*Then she fell on her face, and bowed herself to the ground, and said unto him, Why have I found grace in thy eyes, that thou shouldest take knowledge of me, seeing that I am a stranger?*

*And Boaz answered...it hath been fully showed me, all that thou hast done unto thy mother-in-law since the death of thine husband.*

It was her willing sacrifice for and loyalty to Naomi that impressed him, and inspired him to help her by ordering his reapers to *let fall some of the handfuls of purpose for her.*

When Ruth returned that evening, Naomi was impressed with the amount Ruth had gleaned. Upon learning that it was Boaz's field, and that he had offered the protection of his young men, Naomi told Ruth *it is good...*

*So Ruth kept fast by the maidens of Boaz to glean unto the end of barley harvest and the end of wheat harvest; and dwelt with her mother-in-law.*

Ruth continued to be hardworking, virtuous and loyal. Boaz's charity was attractive to Ruth, but she didn't act on that attraction until the end of harvest. A loyal and obedient daughter-in-law, she then did exactly as Naomi directed.

It may have been her appearance that first got Boaz's attention, but it was her virtuous kindness that kept it, and made him want to marry her.

Their marriage, which could not have taken place had not Naomi suffered famine, widowhood, and the death of her sons, brought Naomi great joy and Israel a great hero.

Ruth's loyalty to Naomi was rewarded, and Naomi's loyalty to God was rewarded.[78]

Were either Ruth or Boaz still alive when their great-grandson David was an impressionable child? We do not know.

But we do know their story would have been featured prominently in the all-important family history.

# LESSON THIRTY-THREE
## Discover Your Inner Eagle!

*When Israel was greatly impoverished because of the Midianites*[79], *God sent an angel to talk to Gideon. The angel addressed him as a Mighty Man of Valor.*[80]

Gideon was furtively threshing *wheat by the wine press to hide it from the Midianites*[81]; he didn't act or feel like a valiant warrior.

Gideon complained that formerly God had been generous with Israel *"but now the Lord hath forsaken us, and delivered us into the hands of the Midianites.*[82]*"*

*And the Lord looked upon him, and said go in this thy might, and thou shall save Israel from the hand of the Midianites:* **have I not sent thee?**[83]

Gideon "knew" himself to be the least member of a lowly family, hardly someone worth sending.

God understood the first step in transforming Gideon into a mighty leader of men was to first make Gideon believe in himself, to have confidence in his self-worth as God's agent.

First, a small miracle to show Gideon he wasn't crazy, God's angel really was talking to him.

Secondly, God gave Gideon a dangerous but physically simple task: tear down Baal's alter and cut down the grove of trees sacred to Baal worshippers.

Gideon used that timber to burn a sacrifice to God. This not only reinforced in Gideon's mind that he could attack the false god of the Midianites, but it also inspired thousands of Gideon's country men to respond to his trumpet call.

Thirdly, Gideon was again given small miracles to reassure him the voice he heard was real.

Gideon no longer saw himself as a quivering, cowardly barnyard chicken. God had transformed him into an avenging eagle!

Gideon sounded his trumpet call to war

Thousands of men responded, stood tall and shouted, "We will follow you!".

Just like Gideon needed quality soldiers, we need profitable employees who can soar like eagles.

If you feel like a turkey, you won't attract eagles.

When we seek new employees, it is important to first value our own self-worth.

We must prove our worth to ourselves with both deeds and prayer before we can ask others to follow us.

Personal Experience:

There were not enough hours in the day for my husband and I to do everything. We needed to hire a vacuum repairman.

It takes excellent analytical skills and attention to detail to repair vacuums. We needed to hire someone intelligent, ambitious, polite, clean...why would someone so valuable come work for our little shop?

Because of my turkey attitude, I got turkey employees.

They took long personal phone calls while getting paid by the hour. Some didn't take the level of vacuum cleanliness

I wanted seriously. Others showed up late more often than not.

I complained to a friend, then added, "Given the job, how can I expect anything better?"

He asked me if I felt degraded while fixing a vacuum. "No."

He asked if any of my employees were forced to work for me, or if they needed to earn an honest paycheck?

"They need money."

He then asked, "If someone's work performance isn't up to standard, is his paycheck honest?"

"No."

I suddenly realized my turkey attitude had attracted turkey behavior. I needed to become eagle-like.

Our business provides a needed service to the community. Customers often thank me for being in business. It was time to share that knowledge with my employees.

I told my repairmen about families that were able to afford new school clothes because of money saved getting their old vacuum fixed. We work for more than a paycheck; we help others live better.


I was lucky.

My employees' old turkey behavior hid the fledging eagles they really were.

But not one of them became better until **my** attitude changed

# LESSON THIRTY-FOUR
## Gideon's Lean, Mean Fighting Machine

Only thirty two thousand men answered Gideon's call for fighting men. The Midianite enemy was larger, better armed, and had a camel cavalry.

The only logical response?

Call for more volunteers!

*And the Lord said unto Gideon, the people that are with thee are too many...therefore...proclaim Whosoever is fearful and afraid, let him return and depart early. ...and twenty-two thousand returned early, and there remained ten thousand.*[84]

The soldiers dominated by fear outnumbered those focused on victory two to one. Moods are contagious. Without that voluntary winnowing, if a soldier asked another, "What to you think our chances of winning are?" there would have been a two to one chance the response would have been, "Slim to none!"

Anxieties reinforced become full-fledged fears.

Fear destroys the will to attack.

This is as true in business as it is on the battlefield.

*And the Lord said...the people are yet too many; and I will try them...*[85]

The remaining ten thousand parched men then drank from a river. All bent down to drink, except for a mere three hundred who, squatting in an upright manner, cupped the water in their hands; bringing it up to their mouths to drink.

*And the Lord said...by the three hundred...will I save you.*[86]

From thousands to only three hundred!

Before God weeded out the undesirables, the chance of two superior soldiers meeting each other would have been over seven hundred to one. Their positive attitudes would have been swallowed up in a sea of careless negativity.

Compare God's wise selectivity, with the opposing army's massive recruitment, which was *like grasshoppers for multitude; and their camels were without number.*[87]

God ordered Gideon to spy on the fearsome horde.

Gideon stealthily spied on their huge encampment.

He discovered the enemy soldiers were terrified of the coming battle. They even interpreted their dreams the most pessimistic way possible.

That night, Gideon returned with his three hundred, determined, alert soldiers.

With loud war cries, ram-horn trumpets, noise-makers, and lit lamps, they burst out of the darkness onto the unsuspecting camp. With rumors flying, the entire enemy *ran, cried and fled.* [88]

Gideon's small troop chased the retreating army. Within twenty-four hours Gideon's three hundred defeated the Midianite's many thousands.

Someone with massive ability but poor attitude will fail because he is predisposed to see failure, just as the Midianites were predisposed to see a phantom army.

Intellectual cowards will run from what is really an opportunity, and encourage others to do the same.

Worse, "whiners" breed discord. *Cast out the scorner, and...strife and reproach shall cease.*[89]

A bloated payroll reduces the ability of your star performers.

It doesn't just cost money, it costs talent.

# LESSON THIRTY-FIVE
## It shall be written

Quality Employees deserve Quality guidance.

We should never expect even the best, most eagle-like employees to be able to deduce all our beliefs, procedures and values.

Nor should we expect perfect memories.

Just like in school, where none of us got 100 per cent on *every* test, no employee is going to remember everything, every time.

Written instructions will make it easier for both you and your employees to fly like eagles.

Complicated rules should have explanations so there is no question about what it means to follow not just the letter but the spirit of the law.

The Ten Commandments are an excellent example of rule writing.

Each of the first four contains not just the rule, but a detailed explanation why the rule is important.

Inherently simple rules avoid excess verbiage, as in "Thou shalt not steal."

Later, when giving detailed daily rules, the same principles are followed. For example:

*Thou shalt neither vex a stranger or oppress him: for ye were strangers in the land of Egypt.*[90]

Consequences should be explicitly spelled out.   Rules without consequences are just suggestions.

God does not believe in mincing words; we should be equally bold.

# LESSON THIRTY-SIX
## Your Store: A Stage for a Great Performance!

When Israel the nation was only a few families, it was difficult to keep everyone sold on the idea of becoming a holy people.

When Israel the nation left Egypt, the few families had grown to over a million people. The task of selling "Be Holy" became a million times harder.

Moses needed something a million times more persuasive than the old business-as-usual methods.

The first change: The Tabernacle
This was no ordinary tent. It was made of superior material, specific woods, and intricate construction details. Within it was another partitioned area that was even more elaborate, the Holy of Holies.

The next change: A High Priest
The Levites had already been singled out for special treatment and duties. Now the most important Levite had a new layer of difference.

When the ordinary Israelite entered the tabernacle, he saw a beautiful, exotic and clean environment. Then he would see the high priest dressed in blue and purple and scarlet; an ephod of gold, blue, purple and scarlet; with wire of gold woven in. Onyx stones were enclosed in gold. Rows of precious and semi-precious stones adorned his breastplate.

Each Israelite knew without being told that this was no ordinary place; the high priest was no ordinary man.

God did not need the tabernacle, or a dressed-to-the-nines high priest, but his Chosen People did. Moses could have talked all day, and not conveyed the feeling just walking near the tabernacle gave.

The tabernacle and its associated rituals set the stage for Moses to (repeatedly) sell the people on the business of being holy and to teach about God. God commanded it be built because He knows how much our environment affects our attitude.

No human business will ever be as valuable as preparing for the coming of Christ, but the lesson still applies.

If your business involves first hand interactions with your customers, you are on stage from the first "Hello" to the time you separate.

Whenever anyone enters your store, he is entering your theater. Everyone in your store is a performer; everything in it is a prop for the action that will take place. Every item, from paper clips on the floor to spots on the ceiling, will influence how people see you and your business.

The first thing to worry about is its cleanliness.

*I went by the field of the slothful...it was all over grown with weeds....the stone wall ...broken down...a little slumber... so shall thy poverty come...as an armed man.*[91]

If people are allowed to trash their work environment, they will think of their activities in it as trash. Physically dirty establishments are associated with either going out of business or of being of questionable standing.

It is no wonder that another term for "shabby" is "seedy", a place that has not only "gone to seed", but is so full of dirt seed can take root there.

Another part of a theatrical production is wardrobe.

The military, baseball teams, even the girl scouts, have uniforms. Uniforms increase a sense of belonging, especially when they have to be earned. They tell the public, "This person is special."

Even without shop uniforms, clothing choice tells the world how you want to be seen.

*And unto the Jews I became as a Jew...to them that are under the law, as under the law...to them that are without law, as without law...I am made all things to all men, that I might by all means save some*[92].

Paul understood that it was easier to persuade people—to do business with them—if his audience perceived a commonality with him.

Likewise, your customers will feel more at ease with your staff if they perceive you and your employees as being like themselves.

One of the easiest ways to show commonality with your clients, is to dress like the people with whom you most want to do business.

Politicians know this. That's why they wear cowboy hats in Texas and baseball caps in Minnesota.

You have a spotless, attractive business location.

You and your staff are dressed for success.

The third thing a stage production needs is a script. It can be broad, general directions, or detailed.

You must decide what it is you want people to know about your business. Then you must share that knowledge with both employees and customers. Just like Aaron needed Moses to reveal the Lord's message, your employees need you.

Each customer deserves the best performance you and your staff can give.

A person attending a Broadway play doesn't care if the leading lady has a headache or the villain a cold; he only cares if he gets is money's worth of entertainment. He will tell everyone if his experience was bad, or exceptionally good.

Mediocre is forgotten.

Likewise, your customer deserves a happy experience at your business. If he leaves feeling that he got his money's worth and more, he will, without being asked, recommend you to others.

Bad experiences will be relived with everyone he thinks he can con into sharing his pain.

Blah, ho-hum shopping is forgotten even faster than boring shows.


The tabernacle helped Moses and Aaron become more effective teachers. Delivering your pitch from the right setting will help your message to be heard and enjoyed.

The more your message is enjoyed, the greater the likelihood you will receive the lifeblood of all business: Word of Mouth Advertising!

# LESSON THIRTY-SEVEN

## "If I told you once, I told you a thousand times..."

The Ten Commandments appear in the Bible several times both before and after Moses came down from the mountain.

You would think that once would be enough, but God didn't think so.

If even God felt it necessary to repeat himself, we should not be surprised when we need to repeatedly repeat ourselves.

The more important a rule, procedure, fact or message is; the more important it is to find multiple ways to repeat it.

This is true for training ourselves, our employees and our customers.

Training customers is more commonly known as advertising.

# LESSON THIRTY-EIGHT
## The Yak-itty-Yak Effect

As every parent knows, the same words repeated too often turn into background "yak-itty-yak."

But repeating core concepts is vital.

Can you have constant repetition without turning your message into yak-itty-yak?

*And the Lord spake…saying…make fringes…in the border of…garments…and look upon the fringe…a ribbon of blue: And…ye may look upon it and remember all the commandments of the Lord…and be holy unto your God.*[93]

Blue threads became a simple, non-verbal symbol to stand for a few hundred words.

When glanced at by the wearer, the blue threads inspired focus on whichever commandment needed remembering at that moment.

When noticed on another, both knew they were part of the same group; it reinforced identity.

Any symbol can be given meaning. In the New Testament Christ admonished his followers to *take up the cross and follow me*[94], What was once a symbol of ignoble execution became the symbol for divine sacrifice and forgiveness.

Large corporations also give abstract symbols meaning; it's called a trade mark.

Trademarks range from the Mercedes Benz hood ornament (fanatical excellence) to McDonald's golden arches (fun-for-the-kids fast food).

Any business can have a symbol, its trade mark.

Be creative.

# LESSON THIRTY-NINE
# Tradition! The Glue that Binds!

*And the Lord spake...the second year after they were out of the land of Egypt...Keep the Passover...all the ceremonies there of...according to all the ordinances of the Passover shall they keep it.*[95]

The Passover was designed to reinforce not only the history of their deliverance from Egypt, but also their commonality as a people.

The Passover has maintained that community memory and identity for thousands of years.

Learning the traditions that symbolize a group's shared emotional history helps new individuals become part of an old team.

When an immigrant studies US history and answers the question "Who was **our** first president elected under the Constitution of the United States?" with "**Our** first president was George Washington." it shows he is accepting our history. When he attends a Fourth of July picnic and watches the fireworks, he is participating in American tradition.

Your business has a history.

It is unlikely it will always have only the founding members. You want all the new people to feel part of your firm as quickly as possible. It's important for your entire team

(Including yourself!) to remember your business's roots and core values.

Traditions will do this.

Traditions can be created whenever something happens that gave an extra sense of accomplishment, or is fun to remember. When the new employee asks "Why do we do this?" have a company-history based answer.

An employee rule book helps new people know the letter of the law.

An employee Tradition & History Guide will reveal the more important spirit.

It is never too late or too early to start a spirit-filled company history/scrap book.

# LESSON FORTY
## Teacher's Pet

*Now Israel loved Joseph more than all his children...And when his brothers saw that...they hated him...and sold Joseph for twenty pieces of silver.*[96]

If you have one employee who generates more income than everyone else, you will appreciate him. You will want to show that appreciation.

You will see him as an income producer earning every extra perk and every extra dollar.

Too often, other employees will see him as an over-compensated Prima Donna.

Just because other employees willingly "ride on his coat tails," doesn't mean they don't resent your perceived favorite.

People who feel unfairly slighted, often get more pleasure from seeing the company star "knocked down a peg or two" than they would from a mutually beneficial accomplishment.

It is important that any extra privileges are obviously earned.

The qualifications should be known to everyone; the opportunity, available to immediate co-workers.

There is more than enough pressure from the competition. No business can survive if its key players are also sabotaged "in house."

**PART V**

# LIFE

# GETS

# COMPLICATED

# LESSON FORTY-ONE
## Glory, Honor and Dollars

*And behold I have given the children of Levi all the tenth of Israel...they shall have no inheritance.*[97]

Although given a share of all sacrifices and harvests, a Levite was not allowed to invest this income to purchase his own land, or even to pass on any wealth to his children.

Levites were well paid only if the ones they guided prospered. Likewise, no matter how rich a Levite became, he could not give his children and grandchildren a free ride.

Each generation of Levites had a responsibility to guide their follow Israelites.

A Levite had no other way to earn a living.

If ever there were a position that glory alone should have been more than enough payment, it would be caretaker of the very first tabernacle.

If ever an occupation had so much responsibility that the family who held it deserved opportunities to enrich itself, it was first high priest officiating at that tabernacle.

God said "No" to both of those assumptions.

If God felt that even the lowest ranking Levite deserved more than just a sincere thank you and applause, then the many volunteers who do things for our churches, our communities and our families deserve more than a "Thank you".

*Woe to him that...useth his neighbor's services without wages, and giveth not for his work...*[98]

We are individually responsible for paying those who help us. Payment can be any useful service or thing (including money) that we freely give in return.

High Priest was the CEO of the Tabernacle. Unlike many modern CEO's, the High Priest's income was totally dependent of the income of his human flock.

If a modern CEO's income were defined as a percent of what his employees earned, he would be very motivated to make sure those employees were paid as much as safely possible. He could earn more only by finding ways for each employee to earn a better wage. Whenever any position generated more profit, both labor and management would automatically share that increase.

Likewise, unprofitable employees would more obviously reduce everyone's income.

In the same manner, imagine our public servants being paid in proportion to *privately, non-government related,* earned pay in their district.

Whenever a factory went out of business, the local congressmen would have an immediate income reduction. Likewise, growing businesses would generate congressional pay raises.

Congressmen would become aware of the consequences of their legislation.

If unemployment caused governors, congressmen, and even presidents to take pay cuts, then whenever a politician told the unemployed, "I feel your pain." he would be telling the truth.

Both leaders and followers should never be sheltered from the consequences of their actions.

Anyone who is protected from the consequences of his errors will keep making the same mistakes.

If we had followed God's wisdom in how we pay our leaders, many of our modern government and corporate-gianticus financial problems could have been avoided.

# LESSON FORTY-TWO
## Rule Followers versus Vision Extenders

There are businesses designed from the beginning to stay small; perhaps be inherited for generations, perhaps not. Most will stay small.

Other businesses from the beginning want to develop national chains and even an international presence. Most of those will also stay small.

Then there is the small "Mom & Pop" style hamburger stand that became McDonald's.

The details of McDonald's story are different than the details of other American mega-corporations, but the part of starting very small and then growing very large, *that* is typical.

The business world is full of examples of tiny, multi-generational family held firms that "suddenly" burst on the economic scene and grew.

So is the Bible.

Consider the Old Testament.

In the Old Testament, God frequently exhorts His people to learn *ordinances and laws...the way...they must walk, and the work they must do.*[99]

The primary duty given to Aaron, the first High Priest, and his descendents was to *teach the children of Israel all the statues which the Lord hath spoken unto them by the hand of Moses.*[100]

These laws were taught much as a teacher instructs young pupils. The rules were explained, the lessons repeated. Those who wish to study God's law, sought the best teachers.

Like a small, well-run family business, God's Chosen People survived for generations.

Two thousand years ago, Christ transformed the family business into a global enterprise.

The first change, His disciples did not choose Him. He chose them.

His selected disciples became excited, active learners.

An active learner doesn't wait to be taught, he *seeks* knowledge and understanding.

An excited learner doesn't just absorb knowledge like a passive sponge, he goes "Wow!"

The more excited he gets, the greater his desire to learn more.

There is something amazing about learning something both new and exciting: you must share it!

If your enthusiasm has power, the ones you teach will become active learners.

They, too, will feel compelled to share their discoveries.

When active learning happens in a business:

> Knowledge spreads.
> Ideas are born.
> New opportunities are created.

The business grows, frequently in ways the original founder could never have guessed.

The Good News proclaimed by the students of Christ differ from the Old Testament regulations the same way a national chain differs from a small family-owned shop.

In *Built to Last*, the authors James Collins and Jerry Porras found that companies who encouraged both friendly idea exchange and independent learning, prospered more than similar companies that discouraged mutual teaching and independent thought.

A student attitude is good for business.
Active, excited learners are great for business.

# LESSON FORTY-THREE
## Goat or Educated Sheep?

Aaron was Moses' spokesman in pharaoh's court. He watched the Red Sea part, saw water flow from rock and manna fall from heaven. As if that weren't enough, he and his family were chosen to be special priests for God.

Then the first time Moses leaves him alone with the tribes of Israel, Aaron succumbs to peer pressure. *And Aaron said unto them Break off your golden earrings ...and bring them unto me...and he received them ...and made a...calf...he built an alter before it.*[101]

Aaron had already heard the first and most important commandment: *"I am the Lord thy God,... thou shalt have no other gods before me."*[102]

He knew that pretending an image was a god violated God's law.

Yet he not only let the people fall into idolatry, he helped them! Any reasonable CEO would have fired Aaron on the spot! (As nearly happened, literally.)

When Moses asked Aaron about the idolatrous orgy, Aaron first blamed the bad crowd he was with.

*"...thou knowest thy people, that they are set on mischief[103]"*

In a nick of time, Aaron came clean and described exactly what happened.

Aaron, like all who participated, was punished. Thousands died immediately.

Aaron learned that God's laws are not suggestions; they are laws.

The raw oratorical skills for which God originally selected Aaron, and that had been honed in pharaoh's court, were not thrown away because of a major backslide. Instead, the Lord allowed a humbled Aaron to fulfill his divine destiny.

Years after the golden calf debacle, the tabernacle was built. God commanded Moses to bring Aaron and his sons to the tabernacle. *And thou shalt put upon Aaron the holy garments...and thou shalt bring his sons...and anoint them...that they may minister unto the priest's office: for their anointing shall surely be an everlasting priesthood through out their generations.*[104]

The Levites (Aaron's tribe), were given many special rules to follow, especially as regards marriage.

Almost three thousand years later, one of Aaron's descendents, a research biologist, wondered if he and all the other Cohanim (the term for anyone who can trace his official ancestry back to Aaron) could show through DNA testing they had all come from the same lineage.

After extensive research, he determined that not only did they share the same ancestor, but that there were no "interlopers" (sons who had different fathers than claimed).

The rules have been faithfully followed for all those millennia!

According to Hollywood, that much faithfulness is a bigger miracle than the parting of the Red Sea. Perhaps "sophisticated" Hollywood underestimates what it means to be an adult.

All acknowledged errors are learning experiences. The bigger the error, the more learning that is possible.

If we immediately dismiss someone who has just made a colossal error, someone else will get the benefit of our employee's expensive educational experience. All we will have to show for it, is the bill.

How to tell if an employee is a goat to be fired or an educated sheep to be admired?

Use God's test.

Give him a chance to fully admit his wrong doing. Don't tell him what to say, how to apologize; let his own words and actions redeem or condemn him.

Then act decisively.

# LESSON FORTY-FOUR
## You are as rich as you feel.

Pennies shared trump dollars hoarded.

*And when ye reap the harvest, thou shalt not wholly reap the corners...thou shalt leave them for the poor and the stranger.*[105]

This is commanded gift giving; it is over and above any church tithing.

In modern America, there are few literal examples of leaving "harvest corners" behind, but there are other examples of businesses sharing "harvest corners":

> A bakery donating day old bread to a soup kitchen.

> An appliance store donating working but damaged merchandise to needy families.

> A newspaper donating extra copies to a school.

Answering needs in your community changes the way you see yourself.

When you share, you are recognizing you have been blessed with more than you need.

You have an abundance.

You focus on your achievements, not on unmet goals.

In the book <u>Rich Dad, Poor Dad,</u> Robert Kiyosaki described how, when children, he and his best friend worked for free for his friend's father. Robert's father (Poor Dad) thought the rich man was taking advantage of the young, grade-school boys and suggested they demand pay or quit.

Robert kept working for free because he was having fun (Fun can be payment.), and because his friend's rich father (Rich Dad) had instructed the boys that **working for free was the secret to becoming wealthy.**

Because the boys were both focused outward, they soon saw an opportunity to develop their own business, and create wealth. They ended up earning more, and having a greater sense of accomplishment, than if the rich father had paid them.

Years later when the adult Mr. Kiyosaki struggled to become a salesman, he again followed Rich Dad's advice.

The more he struggled, the more Mr. Kiyosaki found ways to work for free for his favorite charity. Not only was he not making any money selling for his employer, but Kiyosaki's donated selling time generated no revenue for the charity.

If Rich Dad's advice—working for free creates wealth—were true; Kiyosaki should have been richer than an oil sheik. He was broke.

Any unbiased outsider would assume Mr. Kiyosaki would be depressed.

Instead, Mr. Kiyosaki felt inspired.

He saw himself as full of so much personal abundance he had time left over to help others! Mr. Kiyosaki felt thankful for the opportunities to develop his selling skills given him every time he attempted to raise money for the charity.

Just like when he was a child, the time Mr. Kiyosaki spent working for free opened his mind to financial success.

Too many people blind themselves to opportunity because they believe "only successful people" have a real chance to take advantage of good fortune. They tell themselves, "I am so needy that I have no time or energy left over to help anyone else."

Being self-blinded, those who see themselves as unable to help others **never** fully learn of their own abilities.

*...remember the words of the Lord Jesus...It is more blessed to give than to receive.*[106]

How many of Paul's listeners realized that the rewards and blessings of giving begin immediately right here on earth?

# LESSON FORTY-FIVE
# Mighty Oak Trees from Little Acorns Grow.

Just like skyscrapers need deep foundations, truly great success requires strong roots.

God's opinion of "get-rich-quick" schemes?

*He that hasteth to be rich hath an evil eye, and considereth not that poverty shall come upon him.* [107]

God promised Abram, who was to become Abraham, that he would become a great nation.

God waited until Abraham was in his nineties before making him a father. Then, through the two most important women in his life, gave him only one son each.

After the death of his wife Sarah, Abraham married again.

This second marriage gave him a larger, and largely forgotten, family. His second wife's six children are "fruitful" and to a human observer would surely be a more promising beginning if Abraham were to have descendents more numerous than the stars.

Only the two older sons of Hagar and Sarah are identified as the father of great nations.

The greatest man who ever lived did not start out in magnificent glory.

He started as an infant.

He waited until He was in His thirties before starting His real work.

He had a scant three years to develop His business; had few loyal followers, and abruptly died.

A small beginning.

His church has grown.

# LESSON FORTY-SIX
## The Fickle Finger of Fame

Through His agents Moses and Aaron, God delivered His Chosen Nation out of Egypt, and, as if that weren't enough, arranged to have the Egyptian army destroyed while the Israelites watched.

The people were overwhelmingly thankful. New songs were created celebrating God's greatness; everyone loved Him and His two agents Moses and Aaron.

Each time a problem arose, the same people who were going to be thankful forever had *murmurings...against the Lord.*[108]

If God's goal were to be popular, He would have made sure everything stayed perfect.

God's goal was not to be the ultimate sugar daddy; it was to deliver a worthy Chosen People to the Promised Land.

If ordinary people won't let God rest on his laurels, they won't let us either. If you work for the continuous thanks and praise of your fellow man, you will be disappointed.

Gratitude has no memory, and popularity is a fragile vessel.

If you work towards a goal, then you must measure success not by someone's ephemeral appreciation, but by progress to your destination.

143

All successful businesses depend on solving someone's problem well enough that he is willing to pay for your solution.

People will pay to have their boredom relieved (movies, music, books), bellies fed (grocery store, restaurants), forget their pain (more entertainment, alcohol, Novocain), even to keep warm (power companies).

The greater your problem solving, the more people will admire and appreciate you.

You can bank any money admiring people pay you.

It is too bad that gratitude can't be put into a savings account.

# LESSON FORTY-SEVEN
## Easy Street Landmines

*And Abram went out of Egypt...and Lot also...the land was not able to bear them...for their substance was so great... there was strife between the herdsmen of Abram's cattle and Lot's cattle.*[109]

To avoid having irreconcilable conflicts, Lot and Abram agreed to split up, each with his own territory.

Choosing first, Lot claimed the rich grazing lands around the two cities Sodom and Gomorrah.

Once there, Lot spent little time out in the fields with his herds; that was left to his servants. Instead, he and his family enjoyed the luxury of a vibrant, prosperous, easy-living city.

Sodom and Gomorrah's wealth attracted raiders. The attackers looted the buildings and captured everyone not murdered during the attack.

Lot, his family and his neighbors were on their way to the slave markets.

Abram lived in a harsher environment. He knew he was personally responsible for protecting his family, servants and massive herds of cattle. Instead of sitting in a city, enjoying luxury, Abram invested in what it took to be not just a wondering herder, but a strength in the land.

If he had done otherwise, his response to Lot's enslavement would not have been possible.

Abram armed three hundred eighteen *trained servants, chased the marauders, rescued all the goods, and also brought back his nephew Lot, and all his goods, and the women also, and the people.* [110]

The cities of Sodom and Gomorrah did not learn, and remained decadent.

God destroyed them.

Lot and his two daughters escaped with the clothes on their backs; Lot's great wealth vanished in the dust of those cities.

Abraham's harsher life generated greater wealth and security.

# LESSON FORTY-EIGHT
## Prosperity's Preposterous Mask

What do all of these people have in common?

> The average Egyptian farmer during the seventh year of plenty.

> Lot, sitting in the gates of Sodom, observing two strange men approach the city—men he recognized as angels.

> The prodigal son, finally away from home and ready to let the good times roll!

> Typical American businessmen in February 1928 and February 2007.

Each believed he was prosperous.
Each thought he could count on his wealth.
Each felt confident the good times would keep coming.
Each was wrong.

Worldly wealth can put a dangerous Rich Man mask over the person we see in the mirror. Earlier hardships are easy to blame on fate or other people. It is even easier to take full credit for today's prosperity.

If good fortune were entirely due to our own effort, there is no reason life shouldn't stay good. Bad harvests, hard work and recessions are for others, not the successful Rich Man.

When looking in that mirror, the Rich Man mask can hide what we really are, another soul in desperate need of God's grace.

The prodigal son can easily be forgiven his foolishness; he was inexperienced in the ways of the world. He soon learned *riches are not forever...*[111]

Just like worldly wealth can put a mask over the person we see in the mirror, it can insidiously make us put imaginary Rich Man, Poor Man masks over others.

If we look at a beggar with pity not empathy; if we envy not admire the more successful; then we are judging as the world judges.

*"...the Lord seeth not as a man seeth; for man looketh on the outward appearance, but the Lord looketh on the heart."*[112]

The masks labeled Rich Man and Poor Man stay the same. The people behind the masks often trade places.

If the people behind the masks can so easily trade places, then seeing the mask first says more about us than it does about the person behind the mask.

If we truly seek *first the Kingdom of God*[113], then our search for God's Kingdom will guide all our initial judgments.

Instead of first seeing our fellowman as someone ahead or behind in the wealth accumulation game, we will see a kindred soul in as much need of God's love and grace as are we ourselves.

After that, we are free to notice all the unimportant stuff.

# LESSON FORTY-NINE
## Love's Labor Lost?

Job was a devout, humble and incredibly wealthy man who both blessed, and was blessed by, the Lord.

*God said unto Satan, hast though considered my servant Job, that there is none like him in the earth, a perfect and an upright man, one that feareth God, and eschewed evil?*[114]
Satan replied that if God were to take everything away from him, Job would *curse God to His face.*[115]

Satan was given permission to take all Job possessed—even his treasured family.

In one day Job went from wealthy patriarch to childless pauper.

He didn't just loose his health, he became repulsively infected.

His "comforting" friends lectured Job that all of his afflictions were caused by spiritual shortcomings.

Very ironic since Job suffered only because he was good enough to be risked. Not unlike a human general sending out only his best soldier to be a spy, risking torture by the enemy.

Through it all, Job maintains his faith. No matter what happens in this short life, he knows that "*my redeemer*

149

*liveth...and though...worms destroy this body, yet in my flesh shall I see God."*[116]

Job repudiates the idea that either wealth or destitution indicates God's favor or disfavor.

Nor does he feign false repentance to curry favor with God.

Job acknowledges that life is unfair. If he desired only physical rewards, he would not care how he obtained his gold. But Job knows that real wealth is not from the earth, but is wisdom.

*But where shall wisdom be found?...Seeing it is kept hid from the eyes of all living...behold, the fear of the Lord, that is wisdom; and to depart from evil is understanding.*[117]

Job is honest. He enjoyed being generous with his wealth and power.

Satan's torture intensifies.

Finally, God Himself shows up. Surely He will just snap His fingers and fix everything.

*"Then the Lord answered Job out of the Whirlwind, and said, "Who is it that darkenth counsel by words without knowledge? Gird up thy loins now like a man: for I will demand of thee, and answer thou me."*[118]

God reminds us that our knowledge is so scant, we don't know enough to ask the right questions. He has all the power and all the authority.

Job again humbles himself; acknowledges God's greatness.

God never explains Himself; nor does He instantly restore Job's wealth. The same friends and relatives who gave Job mere words are commanded to now give him a golden "grub stake."

Job accepts their gold.

With God's blessing, Job uses that golden grub stake to create new wealth the old slow but steady way.

His herds multiply; children are born to him.

Job's faith is rewarded with a long, prosperous life full of blessings.

# LESSON FIFTY
## Do you still want that in writing?

When we want a guarantee from our fellow man, we ask for it in writing.

God has given us a written guarantee:

We will have abundant life, if we have faith.

God never promises us an easy life.

Instead, He has promised that life will often not make any sense to us.

For reasons we will not understand on earth, there will be times of trouble.

There will be failings.

More important than money, more important than a brilliant plan, even more important than other people, an entrepreneur needs the faith of Job.

Is there a way we ordinary, doubting people can develop the kind of faith that, no matter how many times we are knocked down, no matter how many times we are forced to start over, no matter how deep the hurts we suffer; that we, like Job, can say, "Though He slay me, yet will I trust in him: but I will maintain mine ways before him."[119] ?

Is that level of faith available to all of us?

In the New Testament, the apostles have more faith after the resurrection. There are many reasons for this.

153

One, they have seen the risen Christ.
But they had seen the Lord raise Lazarus.

Another was the Pentecost.
But they had prayed with Christ Himself.

Being in the company of fellow believers will reinforce faith.
But the twelve had been together from the first days of Christ's ministry.

There was one big difference.
During Christ's earthly ministry, his disciples could lean on His faith.
On their own, each man had to exercise his own faith. They were children forced to leave the confines of home, to become spiritual adults.
The more they practiced their faith, the more they shared it, the stronger it became—until it became strong enough to be felt for thousands of years.

The faith of Job is available to each of us if we are willing to continuously practice little acts of faith every day.

# GRAND UNCLE FERDINAND'S STORY

We had buried my grandfather.

Several hundred people meandered in and out of my uncle's large home, including many relatives I had not seen before.

It was easy to spot the Baers. One stranger in particular looked just like a skinny version of my grandfather.

He sat on one of the many tall, straight-backed chairs that had been scavenged from who-knows-where and lined all the walls. He motioned for me to come over.

I did.

He grabbed my hand, motioned the person next to him to leave, and guided me onto the chair. His black eyes peered into mine. "You are—?"

"Fran, Winston's oldest daughter."

He nodded. "Yes, of course you are". His dark brows knotted together, as though by looking at my face he could discern my soul. "You are a real Baer. I am Ferdinand, your Grandfather's brother. There is history you must know."

He started talking.

For the next two hours he talked. When aunts and uncles tried to interrupt, he looked at them with stern silence. When one in particular left, Grand Uncle Ferdinand leaned towards me "All true Baers, no matter what their work, are scholars. He does not understand."

I was barely eighteen and did not understand either; but I sat, listened, asked questions, listened more.

He talked about speaking German at home and Russian at school.

He recited Russian poetry, discussed how Russia had created great poets because her language was better than any other for poetry.

He talked about how some relatives came to America through Europe and others through Asia. His family were successful farmers and tradesmen, and at first chose to settle in North Dakota to continue farming.

He talked about why they had left Europe. About Bolsheviks, who "were lazy."

"Bolsheviks know how to take the work of others. That is all they are good for." His voice took a hard edge. "Laziness is evil!"

It took money to leave, to come over, to buy farming equipment. The Russian revolution had created poverty. The family sacrificed to have first one, than another come over.

"The lazy Bolsheviks thought if they could just take our farms, it would be easy to get wealthy. Our farms were stolen. Our money was stolen. The only way for all to come over was for us already here to pay their passage. We sent the money.

"More came. Sisters. Brothers. Cousins. My parents. Your grandfather, my youngest brother, was born right after our parents came.

"The last family never came." His eyes watered. "I sent them money. I sent the money." Ferdinand told their story.

That last family had been successful farmers; made the land produce more than any of their Russians neighbors thought possible.

They remembered a cousin who became wealthy. The Russians said a member of our family could not gain the Czar's favor, but one became the Czar's personal body guard. The Czar rewarded him with ten thousand head of cattle and the land to support them.

"That last family, the boat did not come when scheduled, they returned back home. Sent a letter saying, our neighbors will remember our great harvests, will know we are needed. That last family, they did not want to take a chance on a strange country, on the poverty we had in America."

He held my hand tighter.

"They were never heard from again. I know what happened to them. They were killed by Bolsheviks. The lazy Bolsheviks." He emphasized "lazy" as though it were the vilest of cuss words.

What Grand Uncle Ferdinand said next, at the time I did not believe, because a Social Studies teacher had shared similar stories as examples of government "exaggeration."

Years later I read newspaper stories about Russians exhuming mass graves, daring to learn the truth.

Though my total belief was years in the future, I listened, enthralled by Ferdinand's story telling.

His voice cracked. "Stalin warred with God. If a village would not take down its cross, or a Star of David, he would dig a great pit, and bury everyone in it. Every man, woman, and child. I know our relatives are in such a pit. The whole family. Buried alive.

"Farms, towns failed because Stalin killed those who best knew how to work hard, how to make things. How to grow things.

"Stalin killed our relatives. They could have escaped. I sent the money. But they remembered too much being rich."

Silence.

In a softer voice he continued to talk about the only kind of wealth worth having, the kind carried in one's head and heart.

# ENDNOTES

[1] Mathew 5:45
[2] Genesis 1 1:31
[3] Genesis 1:31
[4] Proverbs 20:11,12
[5] Proverbs 15:15
[6] Proverbs 17:22
[7] Proverbs 27:1,2
[8] Genesis 2:2
[9] Psalm 46:10
[10] Mathew 12:11
[11] Mark 2:27
[12] Exodus 24:3
[13] Leviticus 11:44
[14] Jonah 4:1
[15] Acts 10:15
[16] Mathew 25:14-30
[17] Proverbs 22:7
[18] Mathew 22:15-22
[19] Psalm 24:1
[20] MalachI 3:16-17
[21] Job 1:21
[22] Genesis 6:6
[23] Numbers 16:13-14
[24] From the Murphy principle: Anything that can go wrong will go wrong.
[25] Genesis 24:12-14
[26] Genesis 25:30:32
[27] Proverbs 24:27
[28] Mathew 16:26
[29] Exodus 20:12
[30] Leviticus 19:32
[31] Ecclesiastics 1:9
[32] Proverbs 26:28

33  II Chronicals 10:3
34  I Kings 12
35  II chronicles 10:14
36  II Chronicals 10
37  Genesis 29:15-21
38  Genesis 31:6-7
39  Genesis 31:14-15
40  Genesis 27-33
41  Proverbs 28:1
42  Judges 11:12
43  Judges 11
44  Judges 11:34-36
45  Deuteronomy 12:31
46  Exodus 20:17
47  Proverbs 10:24
48  Proverbs 11:23
49  Proverbs 23:7
50  James 3:16-17
51  Mathew 6:33
52  Proverbs 16:3
53  Genesis 41:41
54  Exodus 18:13-27
55  Luke 7:6-10
56  Exodus 4:10-16
57  Exodus 4:14
58  Leviticus 19:18 (and at least six other places)
59  Exodus 1:8
60  Exodus 1:14
61  Genesis 46:33-34
62  Leviticus 19:16-18
63  Exodus 23:1-4
64  Proverbs 24:17
65  Numbers 13:1-32
66  Judges 8:22
67  Judges 8:23
68  Judges 9:1-2
69  Judges 9
70  Genesis 2:18
71  Deuteronomy 24:5
72  Proverbs 11:29
73  First Timothy 3:1-7
74  Ecclesiastics 3:5
75  Proverbs 31:10-31
76  Deuteronomy 5:18, and other places

77 Leviticus 19:9-10
78 The Book of Ruth
79 Judges 6:6
80 Judges 6:12
81 Judges 6:11
82 Judges 6:13
83 Judges 6:14
84 Judges 7:2-3
85 Judges 7:4-5
86 Judges 7:7
87 Judges 7:12
88 Judges 7:21
89 Proverbs 22:10
90 Exodus 22:21
91 Proverbs 24:30-34
92 1st Corinthians 9:20-23
93 Numbers 15: 37-40
94 Mark 8:34
95 Numbers 9:1-3
96 Genesis 37:3-28
97 Numbers 18:21-24
98 Jeremiah 22:13
99 Exodus 18:20
100 Leviticus 10:11
101 Exodus 32:1-5
102 Exodus 20:2-5
103 Exodus 32:22
104 Exodus 40:13-15
105 Leviticus 19:9-10
106 Acts 20:35
107 Proverbs 28:22
108 Exodus 16:7
109 Genesis 13:1-7
110 Genesis 14:14-16
111 Proverbs 27:24
112 1st Samuel 16:7
113 Matthew 6:33
114 Job 1:8
115 Job 1:11
116 Job 19:25-26
117 Job 28:12-28
118 Job 38:1-3
119 Job 13:15

Made in the USA
Middletown, DE
13 August 2015